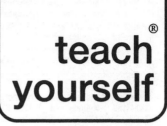

decluttering
bernice walmsley

D0169663

For over 60 years, more than
50 million people have learnt over
750 subjects the **teach yourself**
way, with impressive results.

be where you want to be
with **teach yourself**

Images

Figure 1	Peter Usbeck/Alamy
Figure 4	Elizabeth Whiting & Associates/Alamy
Figure 7	Mode Images Limited/Alamy
Figure 8	Sindre Ellingsen/Alamy
Figure 9	Michael Cogliantry/Stone+/Getty Images
Figure 10	© Alen MacWeeney/CORBIS
Figure 11	© Ashley Cooper/CORBIS
Figure 12	Arcaid/Alamy
Figure 13	Detail Parenting/Alamy
Figure 14	© Elizabeth Whiting & Associates/CORBIS

For UK order enquiries: please contact Bookpoint Ltd, 130 Milton Park, Abingdon, Oxon, OX14 4SB. Telephone: +44 (0) 1235 827720. Fax: +44 (0) 1235 400454. Lines are open 09.00–17.00, Monday to Saturday, with a 24-hour message answering service. Details about our titles and how to order are available at www.teachyourself.co.uk

For USA order enquiries: please contact McGraw-Hill Customer Services, PO Box 545, Blacklick, OH 43004-0545, USA. Telephone: 1-800-722-4726. Fax: 1-614-755-5645.

For Canada order enquiries: please contact McGraw-Hill Ryerson Ltd, 300 Water St, Whitby, Ontario, L1N 9B6, Canada. Telephone: 905 430 5000. Fax: 905 430 5020.

Long renowned as the authoritative source for self-guided learning – with more than 50 million copies sold worldwide – the **teach yourself** series includes over 500 titles in the fields of languages, crafts, hobbies, business, computing and education.

British Library Cataloguing in Publication Data: a catalogue record for this title is available from the British Library.

Library of Congress Catalog Card Number: on file.

First published in UK 2006 by Hodder Education, 338 Euston Road, London, NW1 3BH.

First published in US 2006 by Contemporary Books, a Division of the McGraw-Hill Companies, 1 Prudential Plaza, 130 East Randolph Street, Chicago, IL 60601 USA.

This edition published 2006.

The **teach yourself** name is a registered trade mark of Hodder Headline.

Typeset by Transet Limited, Coventry, England.
Printed in Great Britain for Hodder Education, a division of Hodder Headline, 338 Euston Road, London NW1 3BH, by Cox & Wyman Ltd, Reading, Berkshire.

Hodder Headline's policy is to use papers that are natural, renewable and recyclable products and made from wood grown in sustainable forests. The logging and manufacturing processes are expected to conform to the environmental regulations of the country of origin.

Impression number   10 9 8 7 6 5 4 3 2
Year   2010 2009 2008 2007

contents

This book is for all those friends who need it –
they know who they are.

Thank you to the Teach Yourself team at Hodder for their friendly help and guidance. I must also thank my husband William for his continuing support and patience.

acknowledgements

introduction

When you walk around your home, do you feel relaxed, in control and surrounded by things you love and that reflect your life today? If not, then your home is probably being taken over by clutter. Do you feel as if you are drowning in a sea of junk? Do you spend half your life moving toys, books, clothes, shoes and sports kit from one space to the next? Are you being overwhelmed by junk mail, unpaid bills, old takeaway menus? Do you waste time in the mornings searching for a shirt to go with the suit you are going to wear or for two matching shoes from the heap at the bottom of the wardrobe? Can you never find the things you really need when you need them? Does your home always look untidy? Have you run out of storage space for essential items? If the answer to any of these questions is yes, then you need to de-junk your life and start to sort out all your stuff. Don't worry, it's not as scary as it sounds and you will be amazed at how much more space and time you will have. To make a start, all you need is a couple of hours (or even less), some bags or boxes and plenty of determination to see the job through. This chapter will show you why you need to declutter, and how to deal with the feelings you may have about your junk.

Why do you need to declutter?

Streamlining your possessions and getting organized will have long-term effects. Not only will your home, your car and your desk become things to be proud of, but you will find that your life will develop a 'flow' which will mean that you can achieve what you want to achieve with far less effort and much more enjoyment. You will find that you have much more time. If you haven't noticed yet that clutter takes up time, think of all the time you will save when you don't have to search for several minutes to find socks that match, or when you can, within seconds, lay your hands on your passport or the bill that arrived some time ago and must be overdue for payment.

Clutter makes every job take longer. It is one of the greatest enemies of an organized, efficient life – a life that works. Take any simple job and consider how long it takes you. The actual work probably doesn't take long but the real thief of time is getting ready to do the job. As an example, think of paying a bill. Writing a cheque, popping it in the envelope and getting it in the post will probably only take a minute or two. Or will it? How long will it take you to find the bill and your cheque book? By the time you've sifted through that mountain of junk mail or searched the variety of hiding places you have for paperwork, and then turned out your handbag or various drawers in an effort to find your cheque book, half an hour could have whizzed by. Then you can't lay your hands on an envelope or a stamp, and you get sidetracked by the photos you find in the drawer where you thought you kept envelopes, or by asking the whole family if they have seen the book of stamps you're sure you bought. If your house is full of clutter, this same scenario will be played out every time you prepare to do a simple job. And if it takes so long to do a small job, what chance is there of you doing a major job or of following a dream – something that would change your life?

Clutter also costs money. If you are continually buying items because you can't find something, you are throwing money away. If you buy storage units, files and wardrobes for things you don't need or use, then not only will your home become ever more cluttered but you will be wasting both space and money.

So, there are obvious, practical side effects of too much clutter, yet what about the mental and emotional effects? If we are constantly fighting clutter, we will never be clear enough in our minds to think about what we really want. The day-to-day battle, wasting time fighting clutter, not only wears us down but also robs us of the free time and the peace of mind which are necessary for clear thought and contentment. It can affect our relationships too. If someone with almost no clutter (it's unlikely that there is anybody who has absolutely no junk at all) lives with a very untidy, disorganized person who has clutter hidden in every corner, it is be unlikely to be a harmonious relationship. These problems can also occur at work, of course, and result in poor relationships with your colleagues or, worse still, your boss, and could even result in missed promotions if, perhaps, your desk looks so messy that it is assumed that you can't cope with your job.

A decluttered home is a far more relaxing place to be. It has been said that clutter is the result of postponed decisions. Don't let the decisions you are postponing about your disorganized stuff take over your life. Use this book to show you how to declutter your home and how to make your life work for you.

To recap, here are the reasons why we need to rid ourselves of the excess baggage we carry around with us in our lives:

- To feel better – banish those feelings of frustration, guilt, hopelessness and disorganization, and become energized when you regain control of your belongings and your life.

- To save money – if you know just what you have, you won't risk buying duplicates and, with a beautifully organized home and the memory of all that useless junk that you have had to throw out, you won't want to waste money cluttering it up again.

- To create a good impression – like it or not, we are all conscious of how others see us. An untidy, cluttered home, car, garden and life is not a good image.

- To make yourself more productive – if you are surrounded by distracting clutter, it is unlikely that you will work at your best. It will affect your concentration and also distract you when you are unable to find what you want.

- To save time – if you can find things when you need them, you will function at a much higher level.

- For the sake of your mental health – you will think so much more clearly without all that clutter clogging up your mind.

- To improve relationships – clutter can come between us and the people who matter to us. Life is a lot easier without clutter to drag us down, and this translates into better relationships.

- To save someone else the job – do you really want one of your relatives to have to go through all your rubbish when you've gone?

- To save space – avoid having to move to a bigger house by making the most of the space you already have.

- For safety – clutter can be dangerous, causing accidents and injuries. It can also be a fire hazard.

- To stop the rot – unless you make a concerted effort to clear your clutter and then to keep your home and your life clutter free, things will only get worse.

Different sorts of clutter

Clutter is stuff you no longer use or love. It's things that remind you of a difficult time in your life. It's things that you liked ten years ago but your tastes have changed. It's those uncomfortable shoes that you wore once and can't bear to part with because they cost more than you usually pay. It's broken gadgets. It's piles of unopened junk mail and old newspapers. It's hundreds of plastic margarine tubs that might come in useful one day. It's clothes that no longer fit or suit you or your lifestyle. It's pots of dried-up paint. It's dozens of old lipsticks that you no longer use. It's those piles of baby clothes that your son looked so cute in – 20 years ago! All these hundreds of different things are clutter, but there is just one thing to remember about clutter – if it isn't useful or beautiful, throw it out.

As you will have gathered, clutter can be anywhere and anything. Wherever and whatever it is in your life, it will be causing problems. Freeing yourself of junk will free your mind. It will also make your everyday life so much easier, and the sooner you start to get rid of the clutter, the better. There are different sorts of clutter, usually classified by where in your home – or your life – it is kept, and each type demands a slightly different approach when it comes to sorting it out. Your children's clutter cannot be dealt with in exactly the same way as the mess in your wardrobe, for example. Take a moment now to note where your problem areas are. It may be that your kitchen or garage is full to overflowing or that you cannot find anything in your garden shed – or you can't even get into your garden shed! It could be that your household paperwork is in a complete mess with unpaid bills mixed in with junk mail and vital papers. Let's look at a few types of clutter so that we can see what we might be dealing with:

- Wardrobe clutter – this is often the worst clutter magnet for many people. If you can't easily select an outfit from your wardrobe, or when you do get something out of the crush it is wrinkled and past its best, then this is one of your problem areas.
- Surface clutter – this is where you put things down on a work surface or piece of furniture and leave it there.

- Hidden-away clutter – the opposite of surface clutter. This is 'out of sight, out of mind' as it hides behind closed doors.
- Gift clutter – when someone gives you a gift, they are surely not intending to give you a burden, but if we keep a gift out of guilt that is just what it has become.
- Books and magazine clutter – many of us are reluctant to throw away our books (even trashy novels that we just know we'll never read again), but once read, the vast majority of books are of no further use to us. The same goes for magazines.
- Paperwork clutter – if we can sort out our paperwork at home or at work, we'll instantly become more efficient and less stressed.
- Sports clutter – often we take up a sport (or join a gym) but give it up within weeks. By then we've acquired all the paraphernalia that goes with our initial enthusiasm, and this remains long after we have forgotten the rules of the game.
- Entertainment clutter – all our media equipment takes up an enormous amount of room in our homes these days and we must make sure that we keep only what we use, and that what we do keep is organized and protected.
- 'I'll fix it – one day' clutter – there are any number of reasons why we will never fix all the broken items in our home, but we find it difficult to throw out those things that don't work.
- Sentimental clutter – most of us have got hundreds of photos stashed away, plus homemade items, keepsakes, locks of hair, clippings, letters, old diaries and trophies, but we need to pare them down and then put them on display.
- 'Just-in-case' clutter – we all keep things in case they come in handy later. They act a little like a security blanket for us because keeping them enables us to avoid making the decision to let them go.
- Outside clutter – if you can't get your car in your garage or if everything falls on your head when you try to get a spade out of the shed, you have outside clutter.
- Children's clutter – when we have children, we inevitably collect a lot of junk, but we don't have to keep it all forever!
- Pet clutter – pets can give us pleasure but the accessories that come with them can mess up our lives.
- Inherited clutter – just because an old aunt left it to you in her will doesn't mean that you have to keep it if it doesn't fit your lifestyle.
- Antique clutter – too much of anything can be clutter, so if you have many antique pieces it may be that you need to weed them out and show off the best bits.

- Other people's clutter – if you are storing goods for someone else, whether for your grown-up offspring or friends and family, give the items back and free up your space.
- Absent clutter – don't forget the stuff that is stored for you by other people. It is still yours and it is unfair to let your problems become a hassle for someone else.

You may be shocked by how many different types of clutter you have, but don't let this put you off. In this book, each of the main 'clutter magnets' or areas is dealt with in a separate chapter, and has an action plan so that you can tackle your demons one by one. By breaking down the task of ridding your life of clutter into manageable chunks, you will find that you can make real progress very quickly. In Chapter 1, we will look at just where you can begin this task and give you some tips on making a quick start to get rapid results. You may still be wondering if you really do need to declutter. Not convinced yet? If not, answer the questions below – honestly now – which are designed to root out the clutter junkies.

Do you need to declutter?

Give yourself a score from 1 to 5 for each of the following questions, where 5 means 'more than I care to admit' and 1 means 'none at all'.

1 When you have visitors, do you have to make excuses for all the junk lying around?
2 If you decided to move house tomorrow, how many boxes would you need in order to pack away all your belongings?
3 Do any of your family ever complain that they can't find something?
4 Have you kept any odd socks or tights that have ladders?
5 Do you have books you were bored by or magazines over six months old?
6 Do you possess any spare curtains that wouldn't fit any of your windows?
7 Have you kept any junk mail, expired insurance policies, old passports or driving licences?
8 Do you have any watches or clocks that don't work?
9 Do you have any old or broken items of furniture that you are going to mend or transform one day?

10 How much is in the glove compartment of your car – sweet papers, apple cores and orange peel, broken torches and torn maps?

11 Have you got any photos that you never look at because they are difficult to find?

12 Do you have any ornaments, keepsakes and souvenirs that you have to dust and store but that you really don't like?

13 Do you have any old games and puzzles with pieces missing?

14 Do you save old scraps of Christmas and birthday wrapping paper that you never use?

15 Have you saved many of your old birthday cards?

16 Do you own any clothes that don't currently fit you?

17 If you don't have young children, do you possess any hoarded baby clothes?

18 Do you possess any make-up, perfumes or aftershaves that you don't like and don't use?

19 Do you cut out and save coupons for products that you never buy?

20 Do you have any of the equipment and accessories for hobbies and pastimes that you no longer take part in but that you 'may take up again someday'?

Now add up your score and check your total to see how badly you need to declutter your life.

If you scored between 61 and 100

You definitely need to get to work on your clutter. You have serious problems that are affecting your quality of life. The good news is that big problems can lead to big improvements. Make a start right away.

If you scored between 41 and 60

With a score like this, there are plenty of areas that you can enhance. Read Chapter 1 on getting started and prepare to see the difference that decluttering makes to your life.

If you scored between 31 and 40

You obviously have a few problem areas. Commit yourself to clearing these and you will see improvements. Tackled at this stage, clutter won't have a chance to spread to other areas of your life.

If you scored between 26 and 30
You have a mild case of clutteritis. You can easily clear up your home and your life.

If you scored between 20 and 25
Have you answered honestly? If so, check your sock drawer one last time and, if there are no single socks lurking there, pass this book on to someone who needs it.

Dealing with feelings

The feelings you will have when you are decluttering your life will range from sadness at letting items go to denial that you have any clutter at all. None of the feelings that you experience at this time must be allowed to get in the way of your goal – a clutter-free life. Therefore, before you make a start on the task, you should consider your emotions and deal with them so that you can move forwards.

You may feel sentimental about some of the items you need to get rid of, and therefore find it difficult to throw away any of the 3000 photographs of your children and grandchildren, or experience a sense of loss when you see the piles of baby clothes that your 30-year-old son will never wear again! The key to dealing with sentimental items is to be selective. Choose the very prettiest or cutest item of clothing your baby ever had and pack it away wrapped in tissue in a beautiful box, together with just a couple of items that sum up his childhood for you and for generations to come. The rest of those baby goods should be given to someone who can make good use of them. The same applies to photographs. Select the best pictures, throw away any duplicates or ones that haven't developed properly, or where you didn't quite manage to get both head and feet on the photo. Then put the few you have left – the really worthwhile pictures – into an attractive album. Remember the declutterer's mantra – if it isn't useful or beautiful, throw it out.

If you find yourself staring at the task in hand and beginning to think that all the things you see in front of you are not clutter but are all genuinely needed and that you can't possibly throw anything away, you are showing signs of being in denial. To convince yourself that you really do need to declutter, run through the 'Do you need to declutter?' test again.

You might also experience feelings of fear about letting things go. Maybe fear that you will find you've made a mistake when it's too late, or fear of offending someone who gave you the item as a gift. You can get over this by being rational about the process. Do you really need two irons or two pairs of bright pink shoes? Don't be afraid of offending someone by passing on his or her very kind gift. Accept their gift with the appropriate gratitude – it's the thought that counts, after all – but if the gift is not to your taste or you know you won't use it, get rid of it. The thought behind the gift can remain forever but that doesn't mean you have to hang on to the junk. You must remember that eliminating junk from your life is your primary goal here.

When decluttering, it can help to try to understand why you have collected so much junk and why you are finding it difficult to let go. Our attitudes to what is important in our lives and about keeping these things are often forged in childhood. We are either exactly the same as we were as children or the exact opposite. If, as a child you kept all the boxes that your toys came in, had a really messy bedroom and lived in an untidy environment, then you may continue this trend by hoarding things in adulthood, or you may rebel and create a new, tidy environment for yourself. On the other hand, if you grew up in a regimented home where you were forced to keep your room super tidy or where there was very little money to buy luxuries, you may either vow to 'spoil yourself' as an adult or just copy the organized habits of your parents. Either way, if we understand why we are how we are, we can perhaps take steps to stop our past dictating our future. Knowledge can help in all sorts of ways, and self-knowledge is the most important of all.

Holding on to junk can also generate negative feelings. Many of us feel guilty and frustrated about our piles of clutter. Just ask anyone about his or her clutter and you will always get a confession. Some people will admit they can't force any more clothes into their bulging wardrobes, others will be guilty of hoarding all sorts of useless articles ranging from the cartons that Chinese takeaways come in to tins of food that are well past their use-by date. These feelings of guilt and frustration will build up and will ultimately affect our self-esteem. At the extreme, this will mean that even the smallest task will be overwhelming. The combination of discouragement at not being able to find things, shame at the mess that too much stuff makes of your home, and guilt that you have allowed it to get like this will drain you of energy. Before you get to this stage, get busy. Lose the clutter and you will lose the guilt.

Let's review some of the negatives of clutter:

- Frustration – that you can't find something or that you have allowed things to get so bad.
- Low self-esteem – being ashamed of your home and having to explain about your clutter can drag you down.
- Safety issues – tripping over clutter, food that has gone off because you forgot you had it, the fire risk of too much paper – the list is endless.
- Distraction – having too many things around you can result in a lack of concentration.
- Dust – if things are left in the same place for a long time (as clutter often is) dust will inevitably gather. It is difficult to clean a cluttered area thoroughly.

All of these negatives can be dealt with by dealing with the clutter. When you are feeling reluctant to let go of an item of clutter, remind yourself of all the problems that your clutter is causing you. You will find that the bad feelings you may have very briefly when you are decluttering will be far outweighed by the good feelings that conquering all these problems will give you. Revel in the positive feelings.

Top tip

If you are feeling really insecure about throwing something out, try packing it away in a box, taping the lid closed and marking the box with a date two to three weeks in the future. When that date comes, if you haven't opened the box in the meantime, you don't need the stuff – it is safe to let it go.

Summary

In this chapter you have:

- Made a start on appreciating just how much clutter you have and where you are keeping it. You will have realized that clutter can be just about anything and anywhere. You will have begun to recognize your own areas of clutter and where clutter causes you problems in your life.
- Found out what the effect of clearing your clutter can be – the practical effects and the mental and emotional effects.
- Discovered what clutter is and what are the different sorts of clutter.

- Taken a test to see if you need to declutter. This is a light-hearted test but it will probably have shown that you do have clutter – and lots of it – all over your home.
- Prepared yourself for the feelings you may have about getting rid of junk.

Action plan

You know you have lots of junk and you know that life will be better if you deal with it. However, you may still be putting off dealing with what you see as an insurmountable problem. Don't worry, no clutter situation is too big to make a start on. Once you've made a start and seen how quickly you can make a difference, you'll be fired up and ready to conquer your problem.

Now's the time to begin. Even if you only have an hour or two. Procrastination stops us from becoming organized, so read Chapter 1 – it will give you some ideas on how to make a quick start. Arm yourself with some large plastic sacks or a few boxes and let's get on...

01

getting started

In this chapter you will learn:
- how to start your decluttering campaign quickly
- some general guidelines about clutter
- ten things we can all live without.

Sometimes, we know that we need to do something but, somehow, we just can't seem to get started. We agonize over when we should do the job of decluttering, which room we should start with, whether we should wait for a fine day or do it when it's raining, whether we should find someone willing to help us, or we worry about letting go of our precious belongings. Mostly this is a straightforward case of 'better the devil you know than the devil you don't' because we all fear change to a greater or lesser extent, even when the change is so obviously needed. This is inertia and, by definition, it won't get us anywhere. To break free of this, read on.

When to start

This is your first big question: when is the best time to do this job? The only possible answer is now! Unless you get cracking, the problem will only become bigger. If you can accept that, sooner or later, you will have to deal with your clutter, you need to ask yourself why you should endure the problems it causes you for a moment longer. If you are totally convinced that your life will be better and your home more attractive when you have cleared the clutter, don't procrastinate any longer. If you are not yet convinced, go back and re-read the introduction.

Why do we put things off until the problem has become a crisis? The simple answer is, of course, fear. We fear change. So, starting to reform our lives by getting rid of all the junk that has been holding us back can be scary. We start to look for excuses so that we can put off making that first step. We'll say we're waiting for a fine weekend or we're waiting for a wet weekend when we've nothing else to do. We'll convince ourselves that we really can't start such a mammoth task until the children are grown up, or things get quieter at work or until we can afford to buy new clothes to replace those we'll throw out. The favourite excuse is that we're too busy. But it's just that – an excuse. We all have busy lives, but some people find time to do all sorts of things and those people are the ones who lead uncluttered lives. What we really need to throw out before we can start to sort out our possessions are those lame excuses. The weather will never be just right for any project, why wait until the children leave home when you could do it now and enjoy your children's childhood? There will always be problems at work, and the money excuse is a poor one as the aim is to pare down our clothing rather than merely change it! And, while we're at it, ditch that excuse of having no time. Think of all the things that you might be doing now that are making you feel so stressed and busy, then stop doing those things for a while so that you free up a little time to start your decluttering project. If you do, you'll soon find yourself living a less stressed life and you'll wonder what all the fuss was about. In short, the time will never be perfect so you may as well get going now. The sooner you start, the sooner you will see the benefits.

It is important to make the connection between your external environment and the way you feel internally. If you live in a mess, you will start to feel like a mess inside. Clutter will make you stressed, frustrated and overwhelmed – it is easy to see that you need to sort out your surroundings.

Do you need just a bit more motivation to get started? If so, tell everyone – your friends, your family, the next-door neighbour, the milkman, anyone – that you are having a clear out. Tell them that the clutter has become just too much for you and it is taking up too much of your time and head space. You could even invite them round to see if there is anything that you are throwing out that they would like to take away. Once you've told people, you're committed. If you don't go through with it, you'll look a little silly – but you do intend to declutter, don't you? Just remind yourself of some of the benefits:

- more time
- more money
- more space
- a better image
- peace of mind.

It will help to be specific about the personal benefits of clearing your clutter. Try to envisage how your life will be improved when you've finished the decluttering project. What you're looking for is something that will motivate you to get on with the task; something that matters to you and will produce long-term benefits. This will differ from person to person. Sit back, relax and imagine a perfectly organized wardrobe where you can immediately find the outfit you want to wear. Or a kitchen with clear work surfaces and tidy cupboards. Or a garage with plenty of storage room – and space for the car. Then take this a step further and imagine how this will affect your life. Here are a few examples to help you to come up with your motivation for decluttering:

- You will not be late for work because you can now find your keys straight away.
- You can avoid those nasty letters that come when you've forgotten to pay a bill.
- You will be able to invite friends around for dinner when you have decluttered the dining room.
- You can enjoy cooking in an orderly kitchen.
- You can go shopping knowing exactly what you need because you know exactly what you already have.
- You will feel less stressed during the morning rush because you can find what you want in your wardrobe.
- You will look in your wardrobe and see only clothes that make you feel good, that fit and are ready to wear.
- You will be able to move home free of clutter.
- You can become more productive as you get through more work in your decluttered home office.
- You will feel more in control of your life and your surroundings.

Think hard about your own key reasons for doing the job; imagine the outcome as vividly as you can and you will soon find yourself raring to go. Procrastination is the enemy of an enjoyable life. It is the reason we are in this mess in the first place. We're procrastinating every time we put a skirt that we've not worn for months back in the wardrobe, or when we add a few more magazines to the pile rather than sorting them out. The postponed decision about throwing things out is how procrastination causes clutter.

As you've already discovered, clutter doesn't improve with age – either your age or the age of the clutter. It just gets worse. You have tried waiting until 'later' and it didn't work. Later just never seems to come along, so if you are yearning to live a clutter-free life, the only solution is to get on with it straight away. Today is the best time to put the past behind you. Think about the benefits you will gain, think about the problems the clutter causes you, and then just do it. Do it now!

The most common excuse for not starting the decluttering process is lack of time. But we all have the same 24 hours in every day, so how can we earmark just a little time to sort out our stuff? One way would be to get up a little earlier, or you could try to schedule a decluttering session when you would normally be watching TV. This doesn't sound an attractive prospect does it? Going through ancient possessions or piles of paperwork when you could be watching your favourite TV show will probably not work. You will feel resentment, and the decluttering will become even more of a chore than it is already. What's the alternative? Do it when you would usually be doing a job that you hate. If you don't like mowing the lawn or ironing, then drop those tasks and start clearing that clutter. The gardening or ironing – or any number of other household chores – can be delegated. Who knows, you may even find that your partner or older children are grateful not to be roped into the decluttering and will gladly take the alternative tasks.

The other thing to remember about a lack of time is that we often say we don't have the time when what we really mean is that we have chosen to do something else with the time. When we really want to do something, we will always find the time. Plenty of people find the time to take up hobbies, study courses to improve their prospects at work or to watch favourite TV programmes, while other people will profess to being 'too busy'. What are you spending your time on? Get yourself in the right frame of mind to declutter your home and then you will magically find the time.

Where to start

If you've got to do the work, then it should be up to you where you start. Choose an area that will make a difference to you. Don't be influenced by other people or be led by their priorities. You need to ensure that the first decluttering project you undertake is satisfying and will produce results that will motivate you, not only so that you feel good but so that you will carry on with the project. You may consider the advantages that can be gained from decluttering the different areas of your home.

The living room

This is the most public room in your home and may therefore be an area that causes you embarrassment when people visit. You may have feelings of guilt because you are unable to keep it looking spick and span. If you were to tackle this area first, you would see some immediate benefits and may start to feel comfortable about inviting visitors into your newly decluttered living room.

The kitchen

This is a hard-working area and, if it is cluttered, you will find it frustrating to try to cook or clean there. In addition, hygiene is important here and if the amount of junk makes it impossible to keep up standards of cleanliness, you should put this high on your list of priorities.

The master bedroom

This should be a relaxing area but is often used for many activities – apart from sleep and romance. If you have a small home office area or computer in your bedroom, if you read a lot in bed or if you use the room for storing items for hobbies and pastimes you may see a real benefit in sorting out your bedroom and making it a tidy and calm place.

The bathroom

If you have an untidy bathroom that you have to share with other family members then, by sorting out the clutter and the storage, you may ensure that your morning routine is much less stressed.

The children's rooms

If you find the state of your children's rooms stressful, you may benefit from spending some time on them first. Alternatively, you could ask the children to start the clear-up themselves – with an incentive offered if necessary. But remember that the most important priority should be your satisfaction in the decluttering process.

Your outside space

Maybe your garage is a constant source of frustration to you. Perhaps it is even an embarrassment to you when the door is open, exposing your mess for all the world to see. If so, and you enjoy working outdoors, you may get plenty of satisfaction from tackling the garage or garden shed as your first task.

Wherever you choose to start, make sure that it is an area that you personally will find rewarding.

figure 1 a room in need of decluttering!

Top tip

Take photos before you start. They will help you to appreciate just how far you have come when you have restored order.

Should you get help?

Will having people around while you're involved in decluttering speed things up and make the task easier and more enjoyable? Or will it just slow things down and make it difficult to make decisions about what stays and what goes? Of course, the decision as to whether you work alone or get help will depend a great deal on your personality. Some people like company while they are working, but others prefer to work single-handedly. Which type are you? Deciding whether someone is an ideal – or even acceptable – helper also depends upon his or her approach to clutter. If you know they don't like to throw things out then don't work with them. Work alone. The following may also affect your decision:

- Will you be moving heavy furniture and other large items? If so, you will definitely need some help.
- A friend or partner who is better at making decisions than you, or on whom you can rely to give you an honest opinion about whether clothes suit you if you're decluttering your wardrobe, will be very useful.
- Make sure that the person who helps is ready for the task. They must fully understand that the aim of the exercise is to rid your home of junk. If you know that you will end up reminiscing about old times when you find a pile of old photos, you may be better working alone.
- Having someone to help by taking away all the piles of junk that you're throwing out will be useful. Helping doesn't necessarily mean that they have to be part of all the decisions made during decluttering.
- Someone to provide refreshments will be a big help.
- Perhaps, as we said earlier, your helper could do something that you would have been doing had you not decided that today was the day you would tackle your clutter. Let them do something you dislike doing while you get stuck into the task in hand.
- Having help might work better with a clear division of labour. You could make decisions and your partner could do the inevitable cleaning as you move piles of rubbish, for example.

General guidelines

Here are some general points about starting the decluttering process:

- First get to know what you have. There will be lots of things that you have forgotten are there. Go through your home and open all cupboards, drawers, bags and boxes. Look carefully at all your bookshelves (they probably won't only have books on them), but don't try to make any detailed decisions at this stage. Take stock of what is in your pantry, on your bedside tables, on the floors and in corners — all the places that clutter accumulates. It's important that you don't leave any areas out of this 'stocktaking' – include the garden shed, the attic and the garage. The purpose of this is to focus your attention on the job and to make sure you know what junk you have – do not be tempted to try to start the clear up at this point or to beat yourself up about how bad things are.

- Decide when you are going to start and remember that procrastination is one of the reasons that you have collected so much junk. Start as soon as possible. Schedule the time just as you would a hairdresser's appointment or a work commitment, then set a target of when you would like to reach your goal. Your goal is to get your home into a condition that will satisfy you. Perfection – a totally clutter-free existence – is probably not possible and only you will know what you can achieve and live with. The time it will take you to reach this goal may be a month or a year or maybe just one concentrated weekend – we all start from a different point and head towards a different goal, and there are no hard and fast rules. If you think that you have a long-term project on your hands, schedule in regular clutter-busting sessions.

- Handle only one item at a time. It cannot be stressed enough that if you deal with too many things at once you will not succeed. No matter what type of junk you are sorting, pick up one item of clutter and decide what you are going to do with it before you move on to the next item.

- Put like with like. For example, if you're decluttering your wardrobe, put skirts with skirts, winter garments with winter garments, and so on.

- Be thorough. Concentrate on your chosen area until either the session is finished or you have succeeded in getting rid of all the clutter in that area. Don't be distracted by other jobs or other areas to declutter. Concentrate.

- Don't re-clutter. When you have got an area decluttered to your satisfaction – no matter how small the area – make sure that you never reintroduce clutter.
- Give yourself a pat on the back when you have successfully cleared an area. Celebrate your successes!

Ten things you can live without

Although it must be admitted that it can be very difficult to make the decision to throw out some things, there are other things that are obvious candidates for decluttering. For a quick fix of many areas of your home, try getting rid of the following:

1   Anything that's broken – chipped china, appliances that no longer work, broken cooking utensils, gadgets with bits missing, and so on.
2   Old clothes that have worn out or that no longer fit you.
3   Shoes and handbags that are past their best.
4   Odd socks – where the other one has gone is a mystery and it will remain a mystery.
5   Magazines that you have read.
6   Broken toys, or jigsaws and games with pieces missing.
7   Ancient toiletries, dried-up make-up items.
8   Cans of old paint, the ends of wallpaper rolls, dried-out cans of varnish or tubes of glue.
9   Wrapping paper, ribbon and labels that are in anything less than perfect condition.
10 Junk mail that you have hung on to, including old takeaway menus and out-of-date money-off coupons.

Not only will banishing all these items from your home make a big difference to its organization and tidiness, it will also make you feel that you have made a fantastic start to decluttering your world. Furthermore, you won't miss any of them, not for a second.

Five quick fixes

Still feeling daunted? If you really can't find the time or the energy to declutter a whole room, then here are five quick fixes for you to try. When you see the results you can get from spending just a few minutes on the problem stuff, you will undoubtedly want to carry on. Decluttering can be addictive!

1 Spend just five minutes in your worst area. Perhaps your wardrobe is driving you mad. Can't find anything to wear? Can't fit your new purchases on to the rail? Shoes in an untidy heap at the bottom? Or maybe it's your fridge that is full of out-of-date jars and rotting vegetables? Then don't stop to think – just do it! You will be truly amazed at how much of a difference you can make in even five minutes. Aim to throw things out or put things back in their rightful place.

2 Collect for charity. Decide on your favourite charity shop, set yourself a goal – perhaps 10 or 20 items – take a bag and go quickly around your house picking up items that you can donate to charity. Don't stop until you have reached your goal, and then seal the bag. Don't open it and start agonizing over the decisions you have made, just take it straight to the charity shop. That's your good turn done for the day – and you will have gained too!

3 Fill a sack. Get a big plastic sack and make a tour of your home collecting things that you know are rubbish. Check the list above of ten things that you can live without. This will give you some ideas of the sorts of things that can go straight into your sack. There's no decision to be made – all these items are useless and belong in the bin. When you've filled the sack, take it straight to the bin outside.

4 Choose somewhere that doesn't matter. If there's somewhere that hasn't got any sentimental attachments for you – under the sink, for example, where you keep boring old cleaning materials – then start there. The decisions will be easy and it will still make you feel happy to see a lovely, clear, organized space.

5 Easy clutter – choose somewhere that contains lots of very old stuff that has deteriorated to a point where it's obvious that the only thing to do with it is to throw it out. In this way you will be able to get rid of great quantities of clutter without any anguish and without too much thought or effort. The loft, the cellar or the garden shed might contain just the sort of clutter to give you quick and easy results.

None of these quick fixes takes a long time or involves a lot of anguish and decision making, but you will be amazed at the difference they can make to your life.

Tips for a quick start

Now that you have found your motivation and you have a chunk of time scheduled for clearing out junk, how can you get on with the job?

1 Identify clutter 'hot spots' before you begin so that you know exactly what you are dealing with. Take a tour around your home, going from room to room and noting what's there. Take notes and decide upon your priorities.

2 Arm yourself with a plentiful supply of boxes or bags.

3 Choose a small area to start. If you race around from room to room, thinking that you can declutter your entire house in one go, you are very likely to fail. Decluttering is a little like eating an elephant. And how do you do that? The answer is, of course, 'one chunk at a time'. So, pick a small part of your home – perhaps a corner of your living room where old newspapers and magazines are abandoned or a counter top in your kitchen where junk mail is left every morning.

4 Get a timer. Setting a time limit – of as little as 15 minutes – before you start work on a cluttered area will focus your attention and also ensure that you are not daunted by the task. Anyone can find 15 minutes to tackle a problem that is causing feelings of guilt or dissatisfaction.

5 Invite your in-laws or a particularly tidy and organized friend to stay in two weeks' time. You will be embarrassed at the thought of them inspecting your messy living room or bathroom and you will want to get started right away.

4 Get motivated. Spend some time thinking of the advantages that will come your way when you have decluttered each problem area in your home.

Now, your clutter did not appear overnight and the problem will not be solved overnight. Your clutter and your habits will have developed over many years, and taking control and changing your routines will not happen without hard work over a period of time. You then need to keep up the effort of your reformed habits. However, if you follow the quick start tips above, you will have made a good start. By getting rid of just some of your clutter, you will be able to see some space and you will start to feel more organized. This will motivate you to take the next step. So take that first step now.

What you need to make a start

The good thing about decluttering is that it doesn't demand a great deal of fancy or expensive equipment. The things you will use will probably be things that you already have in your home. The essentials are:

- Plenty of plastic sacks and some boxes. If the things you are throwing out are sharp or heavy, you will find that a box is better, but clothing and paperwork can be stuffed into sacks.
- Some labels, a permanent marker and packing tape. Large labels that can be seen across the loft are best so that you'll know exactly where you've packed away the Christmas decorations or your precious collection of comics.
- Cleaning materials. Junk is always surrounded by dust and dirt so clean up as you go.

Here are a few extras that you might find handy:

- A pair of stepladders for reaching high shelves.
- Work gloves – decluttering can be a rough job so protect your hands.
- A dust mask for the really dirty jobs.
- A sharp knife, scissors and string.

Where will it all go?

You have three basic choices when you have gathered all your clutter together and decided that it has no place in your life:

1 Sell it.
2 Give it away.
3 Throw it away or recycle it.

If you are considering the first two options for an item then it will obviously need to be in a good state of repair. This might include serviceable clothes, any complete sets of games, cutlery, shoes, crockery and glassware, books, magazines, furniture, bed linen, towels, computers and gadgets.

The last option is for those items that not only do not have any further use for you but are also not likely to be of any use to anyone. This will include broken electrical items, moth-eaten or torn clothes, odd shoes, mildewed books, magazines that you have cut recipes out of, old diaries and paperwork, and games and jigsaws with pieces missing.

Let's look at the three options in a little more detail:

Selling your clutter

Money can motivate almost anyone, so this is usually a good option for the right items and it is surprising just how much of the stuff that you have no further use for can be sold. Check out a few car-boot sales or Internet auction sites and you will start to think that 'people will buy just about anything!' Remember – one man's junk is another man's treasure.

If you decide to run a stall at a car-boot sale, you will need to be prepared. It will be an early start so that you can set up your stall before the buyers arrive. It can be hard work, but the money you will have made at the end of the day and the feeling of relief at getting rid of so much junk in one go will surely be enough to make it worthwhile. Boot sales are advertised in local papers and usually take place on weekend mornings. Equip yourself with a table – and possibly a clothes rail – to display your wares, and also some loose change and something to keep it in. One further bit of advice – keep your wits about you. Believe it or not, buyers will haggle over pennies and some people may even try to steal your junk. Yes, the old things that you only wanted pennies for, so watch out.

If you want to give the Internet a try to dispose of your unwanted stuff, there are a few choices to make. The best known of the auction sites is www.ebay.co.uk (or www.ebay.com) and it is relatively easy to list your items for sale here. There is plenty of help on the site for newcomers, so check it out. If you have a lot of books to sell, then www.amazon.co.uk (or www.amazon.com) might be the site for you. As well as selling new books direct from publishers, they offer a facility for the sale of used books by members of the public. You simply list your books in the appropriate area of the site (a price is suggested for each item) and you will be informed if someone buys your book so that you can parcel it up and send it off to the buyer. The drawback here can be the cost of postage, so make sure that the sale price of heavier books makes this worthwhile.

Giving it away

This option is a little easier than the first but can still be motivational. It will be far easier to let go of your possessions if you know that someone will benefit from them. You do, of course, have two choices if you decide that some of your junk is good enough to give away. You can either give it to someone you know (in which case, make sure that the person you give it to really does want it) or you can give it to charity. Take a stroll down your local high street and there will be a selection of charity shops, all of which will be glad to receive your old clothes, books and household items. Just choose your favourite charity, drop off your bags of goods and bask in the warm glow of having helped someone less fortunate than yourself.

Some items may be the subject of more specialized disposal. Spectacles, old mobile phones or furniture in good condition can all be given to charities that can sell, rework or reuse them to raise money and to ensure that disadvantaged people both locally and worldwide can benefit from your cast-offs.

Throwing it away

This can be the easiest option, but you will still have some choices to make. Can the items be recycled? Even very old clothes can be reused in the paper industry, or obsolete computers can be broken down into spare parts. Books are welcome in many places and even old personal paperwork can be recycled as waste paper if you shred it first (to guard against identity theft and keep your affairs confidential). Scrap metal is still in demand so make sure that even your odd bits of hardware are sent to be recycled.

If you're sure that your clutter really belongs in the bin, then you will have to organize that. Don't forget that fly-tipping is illegal and you should dispose of all your waste responsibly. Consider a number of choices:

- Will it fit in your household bin? Take care not to overload your bin (in most areas the equipment used to unload your bin on to the dustcart precludes a bin so full that the lid won't close). Each area will also have a few rules about what can and what can't be disposed of in this way – check this out with your local council.
- Take it to the council waste disposal site yourself. If the item will fit into your car, get it out of your way right away by

taking a trip to the tip. The sooner you can let the stuff go, the sooner you can start your clutter-free life, and the sooner the temptation to bring any of that junk back into your life will be gone.

- If you have plenty of junk, it may be worth hiring a skip – and they come in various sizes. Check out local skip operators in the telephone directory. They will drop a skip outside your home (do you have room on your driveway or will it have to go on the road? Be sure to let the operator know this in advance) and then collect it when you've filled it up. Don't be surprised if people start to sift through your rubbish, selecting items that they want, and don't worry about it. After all, you've thrown it out.

- Ask the council to take the item away. A quick telephone call to your local council will ascertain their policy. Some councils remove items for free while others always make a charge. It will be worth it to get rid of those larger items. How else will you get that old wardrobe out of your way? The local council can also help you with advice on how to get rid of hazardous waste such as old car batteries, refrigerators, paint and insecticides. They will often deal with many of these items themselves (sometimes at a small cost) or will be able to refer you to a local organization operating 'green' disposal policies.

Whichever way you choose to dispose of your unwanted stuff, get it off your premises as soon as possible. Don't let it make its way back into your home. As soon as you've made the decision to let it go (a decision that you may have been putting off for years, don't forget) then let it go. It is not much better to have a pile of books or clothes in the garage, awaiting disposal, than to have a pile of books in your living room or bedroom, awaiting a day when you can throw them out.

Summary

In this chapter you have:

- Learned that the only time to start the decluttering process is now, as the perfect time will never arrive.
- Reviewed the benefits of decluttering that are personal to you. Whether you are looking for more time to do the things you really want to do rather than dealing with your junk, or you are planning to move home and don't want to have to pay to move things that need throwing out, or are motivated

by totally different reasons, there will be specific things that will drive your desire for change.

- Found suggestions for where you can find the time to do the task that you have been putting off.
- Got some tips for a quick start, including identifying your clutter hot spots, choosing an area to start, getting the necessary equipment and getting motivated by thinking of the advantages of a decluttered home.
- Been given help on deciding where to start. If you are doing the work, that decision must be yours and you must start somewhere that will produce sufficient satisfaction from your efforts to make you want to carry on.
- Considered whether you are the sort of person who will benefit from getting some help with the task and thought about the sorts of things that your helper might do.
- Learned the general guidelines of decluttering. These include getting to grips with your clutter so that you know just what you are dealing with, scheduling some time to make a start, and having a target of when you will be clutter-free. When decluttering, handle only one item at a time, put like with like and do not re-clutter. Finally, you should celebrate your success.
- Found out ten things that you can live without – ranging from scruffy wrapping paper, old magazines and odd socks to ancient toiletries.
- Discovered five quick fixes with which you can begin your decluttering journey if you are still feeling reluctant to make a start. You could devote only five minutes to your worst area of clutter, collect a bagful of stuff for charity, fill a plastic sack during a quick tour of your home, concentrate on an area that doesn't involve any sentimental attachments or go for an area that contains lots of obvious clutter.
- Discovered your options for all the stuff that you will get rid of during your decluttering sessions, whether you decide to sell it, give it away or throw it out.

Action plan

In this chapter we have concentrated on how to make a start on decluttering. Your next steps are to:

- Write down why you want to declutter. Find the reasons and motivations that are personal to you.

- Plan when you will start – the sooner the better – and schedule some time.
- Decide where you will start. Make it somewhere that is both important to you and also where you will be able to make a real difference in a short space of time.
- Get equipped – gather plastic sacks, boxes, labels and cleaning materials and dress yourself in old clothes (you can throw them out when you've finished) so that you don't mind getting dirty.
- Do a bit of local research. Check out your local charity shops to see what sorts of things they take, then find out from your local council the services they can offer for disposing of your clutter.
- Choose two of the five quick fixes given in this chapter and do them – today.

02

bedroom bedlam and wardrobe worries

In this chapter you will learn:
- how to decide what you really need
- some ideas for storage
- how to decide what to pack for your holidays.

One of the most problematical areas of clutter – the wardrobe – is kept in an area that really needs to be calm and uncluttered – the bedroom. We spend a lot of time in our bedrooms. Just think what we do there. There's up to eight hours in every 24 spent sleeping. Then there's dressing and undressing, perhaps doing your make-up, reading or watching television in bed. Some people have their home office area in their bedroom, and if you're sick you will need to use your bedroom even more. Moreover, if we're lucky, there are our love lives to consider.

With such an important area, it is vital that the atmosphere is right and that the room is fit for the purpose. If there's junk all around – an overflowing waste bin, a jumble of jewellery on the dressing table, a collection of soft toys crammed on to a set of shelves, books, cups and papers concealing the top of the bedside cabinet, not to mention the horrors of a too full wardrobe hiding behind closed doors (but still displaying itself in your mind) – how restful do you think the bedroom will be?

Your first step to creating a cosy haven is, as always, to assess what you have. If you have too many small pieces of furniture and lots of ornaments and knick-knacks, get them out of there. Aim for as few pieces of furniture as possible. The bedroom always contains large items such as wardrobes, the bed and so on, and there will be precious little room left for occasional tables, standard lamps, floor vases, small, decorative cupboards, shelves and display cabinets. Think what you really need, then be merciless in your cull of excess furniture.

What do you really need in your wardrobe?

Did you know that most people wear just 20 per cent of their clothes for 80 per cent of the time? Do you know which is your 20 per cent? If you have wardrobes overflowing with clothes and accessories but continually feel that you have nothing to wear, then you will definitely feel better – and dress better – if you pare down and organize your wardrobe. Find your 20 per cent and organize that. The remainder of your clothes will need to be sternly evaluated to see whether they justify their place in your wardrobe.

Of course, a major problem when it comes to clothes clutter is that clothes can exert a powerful influence on us. They have all sorts of memories attached to them. It is almost as if the story of your life is sewn into them. You keep the ridiculous stiletto heels that you've worn just once but that was on the day that you met your husband and you know they impressed him, or the dress that was a favourite when you were in your teens but is highly unlikely ever to fit you again. To get ourselves into a frame of mind where we are willing to let these clothes go we need to realize that it is the memories that you need to keep, not the clothes. One very effective idea is to take photographs of the sentimental items (or find them in your extensive photo collection that's just waiting to be decluttered). Then, if you give those shoes and that dress to the charity shop, you will still be able to recall the day you met your husband or the summer days of your teenage years; that won't change – but your wardrobe will be more organized and useful. Clearing out your wardrobe can actually enhance those memories and will certainly leave you feeling more optimistic and ready to move on with your life.

To determine what clothes you really need, you must understand both your lifestyle and your clothes personality. Your lifestyle will determine many aspects of your wardrobe in that the clothes you keep will have to work hard and they must

figure 2 an overflowing wardrobe

suit your life. There is no point in a young mother of three children under five having a wardrobe full of white linen tops and trousers or a fine array of ball gowns (unless she's an unusual young mother!). She needs some practical, easy-to-take-care-of outfits that will enable her to look after her children without worrying about her clothes. Similarly, when your lifestyle undergoes a major change, you will need to change and adapt your wardrobe to match. If you leave a top corporate position to work from home, for example, you will find that the 'power suits' that were the backbone of your wardrobe will be relegated to the 'hardly ever worn' pile. In their place you will be building up a set of clothes that are easy to wear with perhaps the occasional suit for a special occasion. The key to not building up clutter in this situation is to sell or throw out the suits.

Finding your 'clothes personality' is easy if you take into account what you feel great in. Think about what you are wearing when you get complimented, and about the colours that look good on you. Try a few different colours against your skin and see which ones make you look glowing and healthy and which ones make your skin look dull. If you find it difficult to decide which colours really suit you, treat yourself to a session with an image consultant who will not only be able to tell you which family of colours (including make-up) that you should be wearing to make the most of yourself, but also the shapes and styles that fit with your personality and body shape.

You should also take into account what sort of clothes you feel most comfortable in. This doesn't mean that your wardrobe should consist of baggy jumpers and tracksuit bottoms, but it should contain clothes that are 'you'. Some people feel at their best in tailored suits, some in floaty dresses. You need to decide who you are and what you want your clothes to say about you.

How do you decide what to keep and what to get rid of from your wardrobe? Here's a checklist of the questions you should be asking yourself as you examine each and every item:

- Does it fit?
- Is it comfortable?
- Is it flattering?
- Is it easy to wear?
- Is it still in fashion?
- How long is it since I last wore it?

- Would I wear it if it was cleaned, shortened, let out or taken in?
- Is this item appropriate to this season?
- Does this item have at least one other item that goes with it?

If you've not worn something in the last year, you probably won't ever wear it and you certainly won't miss it. There will be some reason why you've not worn it. Maybe you've dragged it out of your wardrobe and then put it back because it just doesn't feel right or you know that it has a button missing. Maybe it's uncomfortable or awkward to wear because the wrap of the skirt has to be 'just so' or the top is too low-cut for your taste. You have a choice of what to do with these items – either repair or alter them so that you will wear them or throw them out.

You only have one choice with items that don't fit you, are out of fashion or don't make you feel good when you wear them – get them out of your wardrobe. This will include all those shirts that are too tight under your arms, all the sweaters that make you itch when you wear them, all the impulse buys that just aren't your colour and all the mini-skirts that you're waiting to come back into fashion again.

If you're decluttering your wardrobe in July and you can't see the summer dresses for a mound of heavy sweaters and coats or vice-versa in winter, then you need to separate the seasons in your clothing – the next section covers this in more detail.

Take note as you're going through your clothing of what goes with what. Every skirt or pair of trousers should have more than one top that you are happy to wear with them and each dress should have shoes that are suited to the outfit. If you find items that do not have a match – a skirt in a colour that just doesn't go with any of your blouses or sweaters, for example – then get it out of your wardrobe. Don't be tempted to go out shopping in the hope of finding just the right matching item. This will only result in you spending more money and in packing your wardrobe even tighter with clothes. Learn from your mistakes.

Now, you have made some decisions and you should have ended up with three piles:

1 Clothes you are happy to wear, are right for the season now and which don't need any repairs or cleaning. This should be your 20 per cent or thereabouts. Put these back into your wardrobe; there are more ideas for storage in the next section.

2 Things that need to be repaired or cleaned. Keep these to one side and schedule some time for doing the necessary work so that you have all these useful items back in your wardrobe available to wear as soon as possible. If, when you look more closely at some of the repairs that are needed, you decide it will not be possible to make the item something you would be happy to wear, put it in the next pile.

3 Things to get rid of – they are never going back into your wardrobe. This pile will need to be subdivided because there are a couple of options for disposing of the items:

- If the item is unwearable – it's permanently stained or has been torn so badly that you can't make a simple repair – send it to the nearest recycling point or throw them immediately in the bin. Do not be tempted to sort through such items again. You've got this far and the decision has been made – so let it go.

- If the item is wearable – by somebody but not by you – then pack it up straight away and take it to your favourite charity shop or, if you know a friend would love it, give it away. Either way, someone will have a 'new' item of clothing to wear and you will have more room in your wardrobe and in your life. If these wearable items are really good quality and in perfect condition it may be possible to make a bit of money for yourself by selling them at a dress agency or on the Internet.

Top tip

Don't be tempted to save clothes in case they come back into fashion – there is always a contemporary twist that makes the new fashion different.

Separating the seasons

Your wardrobe should only contain the clothes, shoes and accessories that you will wear consistently in the current season. All of the clothes that you decide to keep during the paring down of your wardrobe which are not appropriate for the current season should be stored away. The place you choose to store out-of-season clothing can be less accessible than your wardrobe but must still be away from damp or direct sunlight.

The options for this include:

- the loft
- an under-stairs cupboard
- a spare bedroom
- under the bed in suitcases or specially-bought bags
- the top of your wardrobe or other cupboards.

If you use bags, suitcases or boxes to store these items, make sure that you label them clearly so that they will be accessible for you as soon as the weather changes.

Having separated and stored your unseasonal clothes in this way, all that will be left for you to choose from each morning will be useful, wearable clothes and you will save lots of time by not having to sort through lots of sweaters when you are trying to find that pretty little cotton dress or short-sleeved shirt.

This 'separating the seasons' task will, of course, have to be repeated at the start of each season – or at least twice a year. After the first time that you do it, it will take much less time and will provide you with the ideal opportunity to declutter your wardrobe on a regular basis, keeping yourself organized and relaxed about your clothes.

Organizing your new wardrobe

Having sorted out and dealt with all the items that no longer have a place in your wardrobe, you must now find a way to store what you have left so that you don't waste any more time finding just the right outfit. Your first step is to assess the quantities of each type of garment that you need to fit into your wardrobe. Make sure that you have the right types of hanger for each type of clothing. The different types you can get include:

- Trouser hangers – these can hold the bottom of the trousers or, more preferable, ones with a foam-covered bar that you can hang your trousers over.
- Skirt hangers – try to get the ones that hold the entire skirt at the top rather than using the loops inside skirts. Hung by loops, a skirt will sag in the middle and become creased in the wardrobe.

- Jacket hangers – make sure you get ones with plenty of support for the shoulders.
- Knitwear, tops and dresses – these are best on wooden hangers with rounded ends to avoid marking the clothes.

Top tip

Care for your clothes by using good hangers – wooden ones are the best.

Before you put anything back in your wardrobe, give the whole thing a clean out. Vacuum the inside and wipe down the shelves. Hang one or two lavender bags, moth repellents or cedar wood pieces to deter insects and make the wardrobe smell beautiful. Now that the wardrobe is ready for use and you have a supply of the right hangers to hand, make sure that you put the clothes back in an organized way. There are just a few things to remember while doing this:

- Put like with like – all jackets together, all dresses together and so on. This will help you to find exactly what you need in the morning rush. It will save you time and prevent stress.
- Within each category, colour code clothes – all white blouses or black trousers together, for example.
- Put the shortest hanging garments at one end of the rail and gradually add the longest garments at the other end. The space under the shorter garments can be used for storing shoes and accessories.
- Don't use plastic bags as covers even for light-coloured, delicate items because they don't allow air to circulate around clothes and they can fade some fabrics.

Top tip

If you have a special item to store – such as a wedding dress or ball gown – either store in a nylon garment bag or in a box with acid-free tissue.

figure 3 a beautifully ordered wardrobe

Sorting and storing shoes and accessories

This section encompasses shoes, handbags, scarves, ties and belts. In this category we will also include other things that are kept in your bedroom such as jewellery, make-up and hair paraphernalia. We spend an enormous amount of money in these areas and we owe it to ourselves to make sure that we know – and use – what we have before we buy any more.

Shoes

Shoes are a problem for many of us. Our feet rarely change in size so we accumulate lots and lots of pairs and then hang on to all manner of horrors 'just in case'. The same principles apply to footwear as apply to clothing. If they don't fit, aren't comfortable, they don't fit your lifestyle, you haven't worn them in 12 months or they are no longer in fashion, get rid of them.

Shoes, though, bring their own problems. They seem to encourage us to acquire them in great numbers. Another reason apart from materialism that we accumulate so many pairs of shoes seems to be the eternal quest for a comfortable pair. As each pair in which we invest our money and our hopes are found not to be wearable for any length of time, we add yet another pair of shoes to the pile at the bottom of our wardrobe. And then we arrive at the other great problem with shoes – storage. The pile grows and grows and looks untidier by the day. Soon it is impossible to find anything other than the two pairs of shoes that we wear every day and which 'go with anything'. These, of course, never make it to the wardrobe as we're always wearing them! Keep these shoes and very little else.

For a quick fix for the shoe pile, arm yourself with a large plastic bag and fill it with any shoes that hurt you when you wear them. It is said that if your feet hurt, it will show in your face. Believe this and throw them out!

Jewellery

Jewellery is another accessory that can bring more stress than joy into our lives. Sometimes, the trouble of insuring it, hiding it before we leave home for a holiday and storing it safely just isn't worth it. If you're wearing some of your jewellery as a status symbol, think again and consider whether you really need it. If you have pieces, however, that enhance your appearance, go with several outfits, and truly make you feel good while you're wearing them, these are the things to keep. Throw out:

- anything broken, knotted up or tarnished
- single earrings
- any jewellery that you bought to go with an outfit that you no longer wear
- anything you haven't worn for 12 months.

When you've pared down your collection of jewellery, store it so that everything is visible and accessible. Don't let it get into a tangled mess – you'll spend far too much time undoing the knots that mysteriously appear in necklaces. Here are some ideas for jewellery and accessories storage:

- A cutlery divider – the plastic trays designed to store cutlery make an ideal container for all sorts of jewellery. These can be bought quite cheaply from kitchen departments or DIY (do-it-yourself) stores.

- Ice cube trays – these have lots of small storage compartments that are just right for rings and earrings.
- Shoe hangers – the sort that have lots of clear plastic pouches and can be hung on the back of a wardrobe door. These are better suited to storing costume jewellery than finer, more expensive pieces.
- Cup hooks – hang chunky necklaces on cup hooks screwed to the back of your wardrobe door.
- Hat boxes – sets of attractive hat boxes are available from department stores. These can be stacked up to provide plenty of storage space for accessories such as scarves and jewellery.

Scarves, ties and belts

Scarves, ties and belts can be treated in the same way as jewellery – pare them down and then store them in a way that allows you to see them easily. A belt hanger will serve this purpose for a collection of any of these items. Alternatively, you could store them, rolled up, in a clear plastic box.

Handbags

Handbags can take up an inordinate amount of space and so it is a useful exercise to reduce the number that you have. This is an area where the maxim 'if you haven't used it in 12 months, you don't need it' is especially true, and you can reduce your collection simply by adhering to this rule.

While you're reducing the number of handbags you have, take the opportunity to clear them all out. Even ones you haven't used in some time may contain pens, old tissues, combs, spare change and bits of make-up.

When you're down to just a few useful handbags, store them – perhaps at the top of your wardrobe or on shelving – neatly side by side so that you can choose from them at a glance.

Hair accessories

Another type of clutter that we often keep in our bedrooms is all the stuff that we need to style our hair. Most women, and quite a few men, spend a small fortune on mousses, gels, sprays, a selection of brushes, straighteners, hotbrushes and hairdryers. Hair must get more attention than any other part of the body, and keeping the clutter for caring for it under control in your bedroom must be a priority.

Your first step should be a cull of the styling products and apparatus. If you have got more than one hairspray, decide which one you're going to keep and ditch the rest. Likewise for hairdryers. If you've bought yourself a better model that you use every day, get rid of the old one. When you've reduced the hair paraphernalia to manageable and sensible levels, store it all in one place rather than in several untidy-looking areas of the bedroom and bathroom. Make sure this is in an area with good lighting, a plug point for your hairdryer and with a mirror set up – then you'll be ready to style and go.

Make-up

Make-up probably runs a close second to hair care in the spending stakes and most women have drawers full of an incredible array of products or multiple make-up bags stuffed with lipsticks, eye shadows and foundation products. How can you make sense of the jumble?

As always, the most important thing is to pare down your collection. This is easier with make-up than with most other items as the question of hygiene plays a big part. If something that you use on your face, lips or eyes has been open for more than six months then, generally speaking, you should throw it out. All make-up products contain ingredients that mean that they deteriorate over time and once exposed to air they will not be at their best. After six months, they should not be used because of the risk of infections and skin rashes.

So, throw out all the old stuff then check what you have left. Four brown eye liners? Two black mascaras? Any number of eye shadows and lipsticks? Be realistic and get rid of all the duplicates. Do you have any lipsticks or face powders with broken packaging? Throw them out. Any colours that you know don't suit you? Put them down to experience (and don't make the same mistake again) and lighten your load.

By this time you should have a relatively small collection of make-up products and you now need to find a way to store them that suits you. Some people find make-up bags are the ideal solution and you should not need more than two – one for all your day-to-day items and a small one to carry with you for touch-ups while you're away from home. (Many people have way too many make-up bags too, so choose the two best ones.) If you always put on make-up sitting at your dressing table, then the top drawer may be the best place to store your make-up. A good way to keep it organized and easy to find is to use a cutlery tray – the plastic divider trays with several compartments that you can buy in kitchen stores – and separate the different kinds of product in the tray; lipsticks in one compartment, foundations and powders in another and so on. This is easy to clean too as it can be lifted out of the drawer, the products sorted and the tray given a quick wash when you are regularly decluttering your make-up.

Packing for your holidays

The secret to taking just what you need on holiday – rather than taking almost everything you own and then bringing back most of the clothing creased but unworn – is planning. You should consider:

- Where you are going – if it is a city break the clothing you will need will be very different from the bikinis and shorts you would take on a beach holiday.
- What the weather will be like. Check out the weather forecast before you go and plan your outfits accordingly.
- How long you are going for. A sure-fire way to make sure you take just what you need is to list your outfits before you pack. If you are going for four days then you will need four outfits for during the day and three for the evenings. Don't forget that some items – a pair of trousers or your favourite skirt, for example, – can be worn more than once so long as you choose the tops carefully to go with them. Make sure you pack the appropriate underwear and accessories. An important point here, don't be tempted to add in an extra item 'just in case' – that is the classic clutter bug's mantra and will only lead to a cluttered suitcase filled with things you don't need to take.
- Don't pack anything uncomfortable – if you don't wear it when you're at home then you certainly won't wear it while you're relaxing on holiday.
- Pack a small packet of detergent so that you can wash items – underwear for instance – and then wear them more than once. This will save space in your case.
- Buy travel sizes of your favourite shampoo, conditioner, shower gel and so on, or perhaps decant the products into small travel bottles.

While we're on the subject of packing for trips, don't forget that you shouldn't bring junk back with you (or at least keep it to a minimum). Don't be tempted to load down your (well-organized!) suitcase with the following:

- Cheap souvenirs such as plastic models of just about any important landmark, ashtrays that announce where you've been or special 'sail away cocktail' glasses.
- Anything excessively cute or rude.
- Phials of sand – that don't necessarily come from the place you're been to.
- Things you've picked up on the beach. Driftwood, pebbles and shell collections all look better left on the beach. If you remove them from the beach, they will leave all their magic behind. Have you even considered where you would put these collections if you brought them home? Surely your newly decluttered home is not the ideal place for them?
- Exotic drinks. Bottles of sickly liqueurs that you develop a taste for in a holiday resort never seem to have quite the same appeal back in your home town. They will just gather dust for the next few years at the back of your drinks cupboard and all your friends will refuse to try them anyway – unless you get them merry on your best whisky first!

Don't bring back junk from your trips – far better to bring back lots of lovely memories than to bring back clutter.

Summary

In this chapter you have:

- Found out how to sort out what you really need in your wardrobe by asking yourself questions about each item such as 'Does it fit?' 'Is it comfortable?' 'How long is it since I last wore it?'
- Learned how to declutter your wardrobe so that you end up with three piles – clothes to put back in your wardrobe, clothes that need repairing or cleaning, and clothes that will not go back in your wardrobe.
- Been given ideas on where to store clothes that are out of season.
- Got some tips on putting the things that you will keep and wear back into your wardrobe in an organized way.

- Learned about storage solutions for clothes, shoes, jewellery and accessories, and how to pare down and store your make-up and hair products.
- Learned how to pack efficiently for your holidays and how not to bring junk back with you.

Action plan

When many people think about clutter, they visualize their wardrobes. If you have a problem in this area, you need to get cracking straight away. Try the following:

- Stand in front of your wardrobe right now, perhaps with just your underwear on so that you can try on anything you're not sure about. Remove anything that doesn't fit you and put it in a bag ready for the charity shop or to sell.
- Now remove anything that needs repairing, washing, cleaning or some other attention. Pay it that attention – put it on one side ready for the dry cleaners, put it in the laundry basket, or get your needle and thread out.
- If your wardrobe is not already sorted into seasons, remove any inappropriate clothes and pack them up for storing under the bed, in the loft or wherever you can store them to make room for the things that are right for this season.
- Choose one idea for jewellery storage and put it into action – now.
- Sort through your make-up bag for ten minutes, discarding anything broken, dirty or past its sell-by date.

03

living spaces

In this chapter you will learn:
- how to declutter your living room
- how to organize the living room so that it will suit many uses.

Living room, lounge, drawing room, sitting room, family room – no matter what you call it, the room where you and your family relax together is a very important space. Your living space will often be the main public area in your home as well, so you will often entertain friends there. It must function at a variety of levels (formal or informal, for example), and will be used for different purposes such as sitting, watching television, reading, eating snacks or even family meals, the children may play there or do their homework there, and you may have a computer there. You will probably entertain guests in the living room. Your music collection may be stored there or your most treasured possessions displayed there. If it has to work so hard for you and your family, then it is obvious that this living space must be super-organized. If all these uses are allowed to have an impact on the living room in terms of clutter left behind, you can imagine the chaos. A chaotic space will never be fit for relaxing in. It will also never be suitable for entertaining your friends in, and if you have got to the point where you hesitate to invite people into your home because of the cluttered state of the living room, then a major decluttering session is well overdue. So let's get started...

Reviewing what's there

As always, you must first assess what is already in the room, what the problem areas are and what functions you need the room to perform. Have a good look at the living room. What is your first impression? Is the place in a mess? Is there too much furniture or too many pictures in relation to the space available? Are the patterns on your carpet, curtains and walls fighting one another for your attention? These aspects can all make the room feel smaller so you could consider reducing furniture and pictures, and perhaps redecorating to give the room a calmer, tidier, more relaxing feel. But before you can get on with creating a new look with wallpaper, paint, curtains and carpets, you will need to pare down the excess possessions in the room. In preparation for this, examine the different parts of the room. Start with the floor – is there anything on it apart from carpet and furniture? If so, should it be there? Is there space to move around the room to access all the different areas – the bookcase or the music collections, for example – and to do what you want to do in the living room? Next look at the surfaces. Any horizontal space in a busy area will often quickly be filled with bits and pieces. Are your shelves, window sills, tables, chairs and furniture cluttered with newspapers, magazines, paperwork, books, toys, remote controls for various items – including the television, the video player and the CD player – clothing, knick-knacks and puzzle books? Then check out the walls. Although you may not think of the walls as great clutter magnets, if they are overloaded with pictures, framed photographs and ornamental plates and plaques, they will give the room a cluttered feel. The aim of decluttering your living space is not just to reduce your belongings, but also to make sure that it gives the impression of an organized, tidy and calm room that you will be happy to relax in and invite friends into. Look carefully at everything on your walls and assess whether you actually like all the different items you can see or are they there because they've always been there? In a decluttered room, everything must justify its space. Now look inside all the hidden spaces – the cupboards and storage units where the clutter may be hidden from view. Ask yourself whether all the things stored there belong in your living space or would they be better stored elsewhere in the house.

You should now have enough information to carry out your next task – deciding on the problem areas. When you looked around the room, was there an area that drew your eye and made you wince? Somewhere that is so cluttered that it is screaming out for attention? Perhaps the floor by the side of the settee, where one of the family habitually sits to watch television, is covered with items such as dirty cups, badly folded newspapers, magazines and books, a couple of remote controls, some empty CD cases and the odd video tape or DVD. Or perhaps there is an area where the children spread their toys and leave them there day after day. Maybe the coffee table is buried under a heap of papers, games, coasters and remote controls. You must decide which are the areas that attract clutter in your living space, then you will be able to devise solutions to these problems.

Your last task as you stand and look around your living space is to review exactly what the room is used for. This will depend to a certain extent upon how much space for specific purposes you have in the rest of your home. It may be that your children have very small bedrooms with little space to store their toys and so some of their toys must remain in the living room. Or maybe you do have a space elsewhere that is designated as your home office area and there is no need for you to bring mail and paperwork into the living space. List the uses – for example, relaxing, music, reading, television, playing board games, entertaining, eating and so on – and then you will be able to create spaces and storage that will serve all the uses.

Assessing your furniture

This follows on from assessing the uses to which your living room is put. The furniture must, of course, be fit for the same purposes. For example, if books are very important to you, you must make sure that you allow adequate space for storing them in your home. This will usually include the living room where we often display our books as a decorative feature. If this is the case for you, then you must make sure that not only do you have sufficient storage space for books but also that the bookshelves can be located where they are out of direct sunlight to avoid damage. Similarly, if your children are to keep some of their toys in this valuable space, you will need to provide somewhere that they can put their toys when they have finished playing.

Note whether the furniture is in the best possible position for the activity it serves and whether it blocks access to other activities. Check whether any storage units are overstuffed and whether there are items of furniture that can be moved out of the living space. Do you really need – and use – all the occasional tables that are scattered around the room for instance? Or would one large coffee table placed centrally be more useful for the way you use this space? Do you have many small pieces of storage furniture that take up a lot of floor space? If so, think about replacing these with larger pieces or with floor to ceiling built-in units.

Consider how you can reposition your furniture to make the room seem more spacious. Keeping large furniture items around the edge of the room can give more floor space, or placing two small sofas opposite each other may leave room for a console storage unit behind one of the sofas.

Clearing surfaces

Messy surfaces make a small room seem even smaller and will scream 'cluttered!' at anyone who enters the room. During your initial assessment of your living space, you will have noticed the problem areas affecting your living room, and if these included the horizontal surfaces then you should make clearing these a priority.

You will now need to make a lot of decisions regarding what you can throw out or move to another area of your home, and about where you store the items that you want to keep in your living room. Start by moving items out:

- Throw out anything that is rubbish. All old newspapers and magazines, snack packaging (look under the sofa for empty pizza cartons!) and anything that you no longer use.
- Pare down your ornaments. All the things that are on display in this very busy, public area should be things that you love. Do not feel that you must keep gifts on display if they are not to your taste or they do not go with the style and colour scheme of your living room; don't let someone else dictate the style of your living space.
- Move things that do not belong in the living room. Take them back to where they belong. You may have to create a storage space elsewhere for some items, such as school bags and briefcases, library books, keys, mobile phones and loose change. Try to store these items in an organized way, of course, near the front door. A hat stand or large hall cupboard may be useful for these items, but make sure that keys are not on open view. At this point you could enlist the help of the whole family. Give them a few minutes to remove their items which do not belong in the living room and warn them that when the time is up you will be binning the offending items (if this is a bit drastic, you could simply gather up the items and dump them in the owners' rooms). This may include clothes, shoes, toys and books.
- Organize what is left. Decide where you will keep items such as remote controls (you could stick them to the sides of the television, etc. using Velcro™ coins or put them in an attractive basket) and any collections or memorabilia. Provide sufficient storage for things like books and magazines and any children's toys that you have decided can be kept in the family space.

Making it multi-functional

The key to a room that has many uses for a family is to create a zone for each activity. If you group all the things associated with that activity, rather than leaving them scattered around the room, the room will appear more organized. You may need to create a number of the following zones.

Seating area

Every family needs somewhere to relax, and a certain amount of storage should be placed in this area so that things like newspapers and magazines plus remote controls are easily accessible. Remember to include adequate lighting so that activities like reading or playing games are made easier.

Entertainment area

Keep the CDs near the CD player, for example, to encourage tidiness, and keep all wiring tidy and out of sight using cable tidies.

A home office area

If you have to keep a PC (personal computer) and all the associated paraphernalia in your living room, make sure that everything is kept together and is kept tidy. Provide adequate storage for the paperwork that usually forms part of a home office. You can buy attractive storage boxes for file papers or you may wish to consider buying a self-contained piece of furniture that incorporates a desk and storage and has doors on the front so that everything can be hidden away when work is finished. If you do decide to invest in a hideaway unit like this, don't forget to use the back of the unit doors for extra storage. Alternatively, you may be able to make use of an alcove. Shelves fitted to an alcove, with a wider one at desk height, can be attractive if kept tidy with some special storage boxes. A sideboard can also be used to store office equipment and files. Make sure that you do not take up too much floor space by stacking up items of equipment such as the processing unit, the printer and the monitor. Always, always tidy up your papers when you have finished working or you will quickly make your living space cluttered again.

A play area

A child's toy box should be placed where they can easily get at it and where there is some floor or table space for them to play. Having toys – and the storage for them – accessible will encourage children to tidy up after themselves. Don't make it difficult for them by storing the toy box behind other furniture. An alternative is a toy storage unit on castors so that the toys can be wheeled out while playing and quickly put away later.

figure 4 a living room with clearly defined zones – after decluttering

A display area

You may have a collection of valuable china or other items that you wish to display in your living room. If so, make sure that you display them to best advantage in a cabinet suitable for the purpose. This will also help to protect your precious items.

A dining area

If your living room doubles up as your dining room, you will need to make sure that the eating area is clearly identifiable as such. It may be necessary for the children to do their homework at the dining table, but all books and papers will have to be removed as soon as the work is finished so that the original purpose of the table can be restored – as well as an organized feel to the room regained. You will also need to decide about storage for all the things associated with a dining area – china, cutlery, serving dishes, place mats and so on. If you can fit in a sideboard or fitted storage in the dining area this is ideal, but the kitchen is a viable alternative if the two rooms are adjoining.

A last point about the dining area – do you need one? If you eat all your meals in your kitchen and very rarely entertain, it is possible that you can make better use of the space taken up by your dining table. Look around. Is the dining table piled high with junk? Does it contain an assortment of books, papers, coats, bags, CDs, ornaments and photos? If so, consider using the space for something else. Push the table against the wall, clear out the junk and decide what other use this space would be good for. Maybe a home office or an area where you can carry out your hobbies and favourite crafts will be what you want. If you provide appropriate storage, you will find that the area is much better used in future.

Storage solutions

The storage you need in your living space will be dictated by exactly what you use the space for. Here are some of the storage items you may find useful in your living room:

- Bookcases. Remember to place these where they will be out of direct sunlight and make sure that you have allowed some space for new books. A bookcase will soon look cluttered if it starts absolutely full of books and even more books are stuffed in as you buy them. Bookcases can become far more decorative if some of the spaces are used for items other than books. The occasional pretty vase or bowl to match your colour scheme interspersed with the books will create a feeling of stylish, uncluttered space. Books are notorious dust collectors so make sure that you dust them and the bookcase regularly. When you're doing this cleaning job, you could also make a quick check for any books that you no longer need so that the bookcase remains tidy and organized.

- A toy box. If you decide that your children will keep some toys handy in the family living space, you must provide some storage where they can put their things every evening before they go to bed. An attractive toy box or blanket box is the ideal solution or maybe a wicker basket or two. It may also be possible to utilize a large cupboard in an alcove so that all the toys are behind closed doors. Make sure that you and the children go through the toys kept in the living room on a regular basis so that when new items are added (maybe brought into the living room from their bedrooms or at Christmas and birthdays) old, unwanted items have been removed to make room for them.

- Entertainment centres. Group all your entertainment items together if at all possible. Obviously, the television will have to be placed near the aerial point and where everybody can see it, but the CD player, radio and the CD collection should be kept close to one another. If your CDs are kept on a bookcase on one side of the room while the player is on the other, it is unlikely that CD cases and the CDs will be put away every time they have been played. This will soon lead to an unsightly pile by the CD player. There are attractive boxes available which are specially designed to store CDs, DVDs and videos.

- Hide the TV – and provide media storage at the same time. If you keep your TV and DVD behind the closed doors of an attractive unit that goes well with your decor, they will not dominate the room and this will give you the chance to choose a more attractive focal point for your room. It will also mean that you can store untidy looking piles of DVDs or video cassettes neatly in the same unit.

- Built-in storage. This will provide an infinite number of storage solutions. You can have some open shelving and some closed, it can be made to fit even awkward spaces such as under the stairs or in narrow alcoves, and it can utilize space very efficiently by being built from floor to ceiling. Use the higher shelves for your most precious objects and for breakable items, as this will keep them out of harm's way.

- Check out some items of dual-purpose furniture. Department stores and furniture showrooms or Internet retailers will have a selection of footstools with storage space and storage boxes (perhaps wicker, rattan or suede-covered) that can double up as side tables. This will provide useful storage for family games or magazines, and many of the bits and pieces that you need to keep handy in the living room.
- A 'this doesn't belong here' basket. Consider having a wicker basket in your living room where at the end of each day you can place all the items that have been left in the living room but that have a home somewhere else. This could include clothing, school bags, photographs, shoes, homework and toys. Make sure that you clear this basket out completely at least once a week or whenever it becomes unsightly in between times. Make it clear to everyone that this is where these items will be placed and that if they are still there at the end of the week they are in danger of being thrown out.
- The back of the door. Some items – CDs or small toys, for example – could be stored in bags or on hooks on the back of the door. Hanging units are available that make a design feature of CD cases.

Summary

In this chapter you have:

- Reviewed your living room and assessed the clutter that is there.
- Assessed your furniture – is there too much? Does it suit the purpose? Does it do a good job for you or do you need to change it to suit your lifestyle?
- Found out how to clear your shelves and the tops of cupboards, tables and other surfaces and organize the things that are left with adequate storage.
- Learned how to create zones in your living space for the different activities that go on there.
- Looked at some storage solutions. According to how you use your living space, these could include bookcases, toy storage, an entertainment area, a unit to disguise the television, some built-in storage, items of furniture with a dual purpose and a 'this doesn't belong here' basket.

Action plan

- Spend 15 minutes in your living space with the sole aim of assessing its problem areas. Make a note of storage needs and where you have bottlenecks of clutter.

- Decide exactly what you want to use your living space for. What are your priority areas? Is it somewhere to relax? To watch television? Or is it primarily an area for you to entertain your friends? Make a list with the most important uses for this room at the top and the less important aspects – the things that are not essential but might be desirable – later in the list. This is your wish list for your living room and should be taken into account when you are creating your zones and introducing new storage.

- Review your furniture requirements in the light of the 'wish list' you have compiled. Do you need it all? Could you take away two items and replace them with one, more useful, item? Do all the items of furniture in the room serve purposes that tie in with your priorities?

- Remove ten items of clutter – now – from the surfaces in your living space. These could include a couple of ornaments, a school bag, a newspaper and two magazines, a toy or two, an abandoned jacket and a set of keys. Easy!

- Go back to your 'wish list'. Tackle the zone that is at the top of your list. This is to you – and you're the person who counts – the most important use of your living space so it deserves immediate attention. Clear out any remaining junk in that area, tidy up what's left – perhaps providing some additional or alternative storage as necessary – then sit back and admire the area.

- Create a 'this doesn't belong here' basket, or a box, or a bag hanging on the back of the door. Just somewhere you can group together all the items that end up in your living room on a daily basis but should actually be stored elsewhere. This will not only help to keep your living space tidy but may also discourage your family from leaving things lying around.

04
kitchen confusion

In this chapter you will learn:
- how to clear your work surfaces
- how to decide what to keep in your kitchen cupboards
- some clever storage solutions.

Our kitchens often become the centre of the family home. A place where many activities such as cooking, washing-up, laundry, ironing, school homework, crafts and hobbies, and reading the post will take place and, of course, it's where people always gather at parties. Because the kitchen is such a well used area by all members of the family, it can also become a focal point for clutter. Everyone seems to have a 'junk drawer' in their kitchen where all the items that haven't been given a proper 'home' will end up. This includes batteries (new and used), elastic bands that have lost their stretch, bits of string, matches, spare keys, old postcards, letters from the children's schools, pens, shopping lists and sunglasses. The list is endless. Perhaps a cutlery tray in this drawer will help you to get it organized – after you have sorted and thrown out all the useless bits and pieces!

As it is such a gathering place, the kitchen is often the first stop when you arrive home. You will come through the door at the end of the day, pick up the mail from behind the door and head for the kitchen to put the kettle on. Of course, at this point you will be carrying your handbag, shopping bag, keys, all that mail, jacket, scarf and gloves. Where will you dump all these things? And when will you clear them all away? The junk mail may hang around for days or even weeks unless you deal with it straight away, so it is obvious that a tidy kitchen demands a system; a well thought out, organized system to deal with life on a day-to-day basis. Before that system can be installed, all the existing junk must be cleared away. Once the decks are cleared, you will be able to add some clever storage solutions to help you keep cupboards organized and surfaces free of the things that get in the way of the work.

Another reason why the kitchen becomes such a clutter magnet is because its main purpose – preparing meals – is so utensil-intensive. Even making a cup of tea will require a kettle, cup and saucer, teapot, teaspoon, tea bag container, sugar bowl, milk jug (and a pair of scissors to open the milk carton – can anyone open those things without scissors?). Then you leave behind a used tea bag, a dirty teaspoon, cup and saucer and, unless you put everything away as you use it, there's also all the things you used to make the cup of tea like the sugar bowl and milk jug. It's no wonder that making a meal for a family and doing the laundry result in an untidy kitchen. Unless the drawers and cupboards are tidy and organized these tasks will also inevitably result in a tired, frustrated worker.

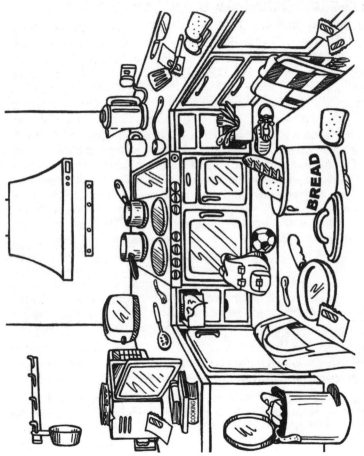

figure 5 a cluttered kitchen

Of course, what you really want is a warm and welcoming room that works. This type of room is unlikely to be a cluttered kitchen so, unless you get rid of the junk and sort out the storage this will be just a dream. How do you go about organizing your kitchen?

What do you use every single day?

You need to understand how your kitchen works for you. How you live your life and what's important to you. Some people will use a juicer every day while other families will buy one, use it once and then leave it on the counter to gather dust – and take up valuable working space. Some people can't see a need for an egg timer – they simply use their watch – but others may view a timer as essential equipment. You also need to be aware of how your dining arrangements affect how you use your kitchen. Maybe you have a separate dining room and would never eat anything more than a snack on your own in the kitchen so you don't need much more than a small breakfast bar. Or maybe you have nowhere else in the house to eat and you usually sit down as a family for your meals, and you will need to ensure plenty of room at your kitchen table.

Do you love to cook – or hate it? This will probably determine how much equipment, serving dishes and gadgetry you want to keep in your kitchen. If all you ever eat are takeaway pizzas, then you will have no need for a selection of serving dishes or pans and cutlery. On the other hand, if you regularly entertain, then while you may not need to keep the menus from all the local takeaways, you will certainly need to find somewhere to store your best dinner service. You are also more likely to have a sizeable collection of recipe books, and you will need to organize space for these.

If you have small children, you will need somewhere for them to sit – doing homework, painting and so on – well away from the danger of your cooking area and out of the path you take between storage, cooking and sink while you are making meals. You might also need to have somewhere to store the toys and other items that children will have and will want to use in the kitchen while you are working.

You will also need to think about the other areas that are available to you in your home because these will dictate what you need to store in your kitchen. For example, if you have a utility room where you can keep all your laundry requisites – washing powder, stain removers and fabric conditioner in addition to the washing machine and dryer – then you will have more space available in your kitchen. Or, if you have a pantry, you will need less storage space for dry goods in your kitchen cupboards. Similarly, if you have a general storage area available – perhaps under the stairs or in the utility room – you will be able to store cleaning materials there or transfer some items that only get used occasionally such as electrical gadgets, Christmas items or cake tins.

Starting to declutter a kitchen can be daunting but, if you consider the use of your kitchen carefully, you will be in a position to decide just what you need to keep to hand. Some things will need to be kept on countertops while others will have their own storage areas.

Clearing surfaces

It can be difficult to decide what to keep on your kitchen surfaces – especially if it seems impossible to find space for anything else in your cupboards. Here are a few ways of making a start:

1 Move anything that definitely does not belong on the countertops and is for throwing out. This will include items such as junk mail, magazines, empty packets, old newspapers and other items of rubbish that have been left there rather than being put directly in the bin or recycled.

2 Move anything that does not belong in the kitchen. You will find that the kitchen acts as a magnet for all sorts of clutter. This is, as we said, because it is often the first stop when you and the family arrive home. You will go straight to the kitchen and put the kettle on or help yourself to a drink from the fridge, dropping bags, jackets, mail and parcels along the way. The amount of just 'living' that we do in a kitchen brings with it a significant amount of clutter too. The children playing or doing their homework, someone assembling a model car on the kitchen table or tie-dyeing a

T-shirt in the sink will increase the clutter level. Put all these items in a box ready to be moved to the correct room. This will include kids' toys, abandoned jackets and ties, bills and letters and sports equipment. Get them all out of the kitchen and you will start so see some space on the countertops, and the floor and table too.

3 Set yourself a time limit. Set a timer for 15 or perhaps 30 minutes and stick to it. Focus on the task in hand for the time you have and you will be surprised at how much of a dent you will be able to make in the clutter on your kitchen surfaces. As soon as the bell rings, stop and do something else – perhaps get yourself a drink and sit in the garden for ten minutes as a reward for your hard work. When you're refreshed – and motivated by the improvement you can see – set the timer again and get decluttering.

When you've cleared away everything that does not belong in the kitchen, you should then pare down the items that you keep on the work surfaces. Ensure that you have enough space to work efficiently and keep the items that remain on the surface to the bare minimum. Keep only items that you use every day on the countertops – kettle, toaster, a knife block and bread bin – and find other places to store everything else. Don't worry if that seems impossible just now, we'll look at clearing some space in your cupboards plus ingenious ways to increase your storage space later in the chapter, and this will give you somewhere to put the essentials that you've decided to move off your work surfaces.

Categorize your clutter areas

Now that you've cleared a bit of space on your worktops, it is time to concentrate on other areas of your kitchen. Viewing the whole task at once can be overwhelming and therefore it is a good idea to split it into a number of manageable areas. Tackle each area of clutter as a completely separate task. While you're working on your utensils drawer, for example, ignore the pans piled up in the sink or the overloaded food cupboards. On page 63 some of the areas that you can concentrate on, one at a time, are listed.

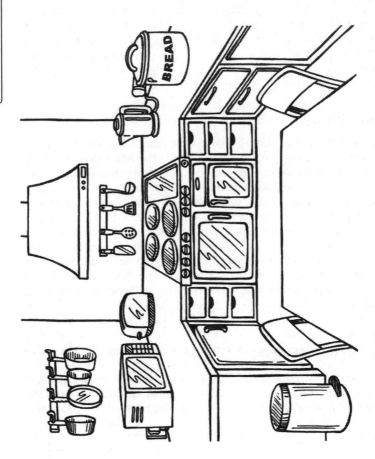

figure 6 a very tidy kitchen

The utensils drawer

Do you frequently have difficulty making this drawer close? Does it contain gadgets that you've used once and then flung to the back of the drawer? Empty the drawer completely and go through the contents. Be ruthless – if you can't remember the last time you used that boiled egg piercer or melon baller, put them in the bin or in a box to be given away. If you are merciless in your search for unwanted items, you will soon be able to slide the drawer shut with no trouble. Don't forget to give the drawer a thorough wipe out before you replace your pared down gadgets. A clean, organized utensil drawer should give you a little incentive to carry on to the next area.

Food storage

This should be split down into a number of areas – dry goods storage, the fridge, the freezer, vegetables and so on. All of these areas will need different storage solutions but they should all be decluttered with the same aim in mind – to get rid of any items that might be dangerous and unpleasant to eat and then to store the remainder in the most hygienic and organized way possible. It is estimated that over 10 per cent of all groceries remain untouched on our shelves for over a year. This is because we buy these items for special occasions – to make a particular dish or for a celebration or treat – then we forget about them and they never become part of our regular eating habits. Eventually, all food items will lose their flavour and some will become dangerous to eat after a long storage, so check all those use-by dates and be ruthless. Avoid waste in the future by introducing an element of stock rotation to your food cupboards. This entails putting new stock to the back of older stock when you're unpacking your shopping. This will then mean that you don't eat the canned soup you've just bought and leave one you bought six months ago languishing at the back of the cupboard.

Dry goods such as dried fruit, flour, nuts, rice and sugar can be transferred from their original packaging and stacked neatly in sealable plastic containers. Not only will this make them easier to find and give you more hygienic storage for these items but it will also save space. Remember to store like with like – all pasta and grains or all tinned fruit together, for example.

The refrigerator

Dig deep and throw out all the foods that are past their use-by dates – all the half-used jars of sun-dried tomatoes, salad dressings, liquefying salad vegetables and unidentifiable leftovers. Wipe the shelves, wash the storage drawers and wipe down the outside of the fridge.

The freezer

To do a good job of sorting out your freezer, you will need to remove every single item. Then, as usual with any decluttering project, make a decision on each one. Meanwhile, you can defrost the freezer before putting the remaining food back. If you can't tell what the package contains (maybe the plastic tub you put the leftover soup in has lost its label) then it's an easy decision – throw it out. If it's deteriorating because it's been there a while, again throw it out. If it's been there for ages because you and your family don't really like eating it, throw it out. By this time you should have reduced the amount you have to put back in your freezer and, just as importantly, you can now see exactly what you have and you are ready to put it into a more efficient order. Keep like with like to make things easier to find – fish with fish products, all desserts and ice cream together in one basket or on one shelf.

When you have an immaculate looking freezer, keep it that way by listing the contents and sticking the list on the front of the freezer with a magnet. Update the list as you take things out or put things into the freezer. That way, you won't waste precious time looking for the lasagne that you actually ate last week, and you will be able to see at a glance what you need to add to your weekly shopping list.

Top tip

Cut the label off dry goods and put it into the plastic container as you transfer the food from the packet. This will ensure that you have details such as cooking instructions and use-by dates available even after you have thrown the packet away.

Food preparation

This is a very important area because this is the space where you will do most of your work in the kitchen and you must get it right. Think carefully about where everything goes and how much space you need. If you bake regularly, you will want cake tins, your food processor and your mixing bowls and jugs to hand. Reorganize your storage to take this into account; the closer you can store things to where they will be used, the more time you will save in your kitchen. Again, you will have to be ruthless about what you keep. Do you really need the baking tin shaped like a figure 4 now that your little boy is 18? Just how many mixing bowls do you need? The answer is the amount you actually use. Get rid of the rest. Perhaps your 18-year-old is going off to university or setting up home for the first time and would be grateful for a set of kitchen basics to get them started, or you may know of a local charity that could make good use of assorted kitchen items. Failing this, the car-boot sale is a tried and tested outlet for all sorts of clutter.

Under the sink

Just what is under here? Cleaning materials? Lots of duplicated cleaning materials? Old dusters, empty cans of polish, damp and foul-smelling sponges? Bleach? Is it just another storage area for little-used kitchen gadgets? Use this decluttering project as a chance to get rid of all the unused cleaning products you've tried over the years and that are now lurking at the back of the cupboard. Reorganize your storage of the things that would be better kept in another room or in a cupboard closer to where they will actually be used.

Top tip

Remember that even diswasher tablets have a 'best before' date so check the packets and avoid over-stocking on cleaning products.

If you have children in the house, move the bleach to somewhere safer – perhaps to a cupboard they cannot reach or to one with a lock.

Crockery and glassware

Get all your plates, cups, saucers, soup bowls, serving dishes and platters, glasses and mugs out of the cupboard and stack like with like. If all your glassware is stored in the same place and all your different sizes of plates and bowls are neatly stacked, you will save time not just in finding them but also when you put them away. Keep everyday items separate from ones that are only used occasionally. If you have a 'best' dinner set and serving dishes, try to find room to store them in the dining room, freeing up valuable space in your kitchen.

Cutlery

The cutlery tray is the ideal example of well designed, practical storage for the kitchen (and around the rest of the house too!) – it keeps like with like and means that you will always be able to find just what you need.

Empty plastic storage boxes

Are these forever falling out of the cupboard because you have got so many of them? Or have you bought various sets of different sizes of storage box and now find them difficult to store and keep tidy? If so, the first question you should ask yourself is 'Do I really need all of them?' Have you used as many as you can to organize your food cupboards and fridge? You may need a few spares for leftover food or new products that come into the house, but you really do not need dozens of them, so be brutal and throw them out. Select your favourite sizes and types, and get rid of the used margarine cartons if you can. When you are down to the bare minimum, keep these organized by storing them in the cupboard in see-through mesh baskets – one for containers and a separate one for the lids. This will keep them from toppling over in your cupboards, and you'll be able to grab what you need quickly.

Pans

Find a large cupboard or deep drawer as close as possible to your cooker to store your pans. If there is no suitable cupboard, you could use a metal corner stand made for this purpose. You can also buy a rack for pan lids that screws to the inside of the cupboard. This will stop those frustrating times when you need the size of lid that is always at the bottom of the pile. As you drag out that lid, all the others come crashing after it. Don't be tempted to use your oven as storage space for pans or cake tins because it will always irritate you if you have to start moving things before you can use your oven.

The sink area

Wash up the pots and pans in the sink then see what is left around the sink area. Only the things you use every day – washing-up liquid, a pan scrub, a dishcloth – should remain; everything else must be found a new home or thrown out. Use a mesh caddy by the sink to store the pan scrub etc so that air can circulate around them.

Your cooking area

Again this is a very important, busy area so you need to keep surfaces clear to work on. Moreover, the area next to the cooker should be kept clear because items could be damaged by splashes and spills. Make sure that you have an area next to the cooker where you can place hot pans without risking damage to your worktop. A pretty tile or trivet are ideal pan rests.

Recipe books

Like almost everyone, you probably don't use all of your cook books so keep your favourites and ditch the rest.

Storage ideas

It is important that you don't splash out on fancy storage before you have carried out the decluttering of your kitchen. After all, how can you buy effective storage if you don't know exactly what you have left to store? Wait until you have dumped the junk and taken away all the items that do not belong in the kitchen, then you will be able to see just where your problems are. You will now be in a position to find one or two clever storage ideas to solve your problems.

Here are some tips and storage ideas that will help when you are putting back your newly organized kitchen items:

- Cutlery trays have lots of uses – this can't be said often enough. They are ideal for storing many smaller items so that you can see them easily and keep like with like.
- Add shelves to cupboards. You often do not need the depth allowed in standard cupboards – if you are storing a lot of smaller products, canned food, for example, put in an extra shelf. Laminated wood can be cut to size at most DIY stores, and fixings will be readily available.
- Try tiered shelving. This will store smaller items such as canned goods, spices and sauces on a stepped platform that fits into your cupboard and allows you to see what you have while increasing your shelf area.
- Under-shelf baskets can help you to utilize that wasted space in a cupboard that is too deep.
- Carousel units can be handy in a corner cupboard. This will help you to bring everything within reach – even the items stored in the most awkward spaces.
- Cup hooks – for more than cups. Use the space under shelving or wall cupboards by affixing a row of cup hooks. You can then hang mugs, small pans, jugs, tea cloths or an apron from these handy hooks.
- Use a tiered, wire plate rack that will hold three or four different sizes of plates in a stack and let you remove any of them without disturbing the others.
- Use a shallow tray or storage basket for all the snack foods that take up a lot of space in your cupboards when left in their original boxes. Take any individually wrapped foods – soups, chocolate biscuits and cereal bars – out of the boxes and keep them all together. This will free up space and also allow you to see when stocks are getting low.
- If you need to free up a drawer, try storing utensils in a tub or large jar. This will not only empty your utensil drawer but it will also help you to resist the temptation to add more and more gadgets. Some holders can also be mounted on the wall, freeing up space on your worktop.
- Reorganize your recycling. If you currently store bottles, jars, cans and newspapers in unlidded containers, invest in some lidded bins that will hide the contents and keep the kitchen looking tidy.
- A mobile workstation can be a good idea in a kitchen that is short on work surfaces. It can be stored out of the way and

moved into your working space when needed and will also provide valuable storage space underneath for pots and pans.

- Install a bin under the sink. Most DIY stores stock waste bins that can be attached to the inside of a cupboard door and the lid opens automatically as you open the door – very helpful when your hands are wet or full of rubbish.

- Look up. If all your cupboards are full, try hanging a frame from the ceiling on which you can hang pans, colanders and other large items using butcher's hooks. Again, this sort of storage is readily available from DIY stores.

- High-level shelves. Appliances that are only used occasionally can be stored on shelves placed well out of the way, high up the walls.

- Hang up chopping boards – a simple, plastic-covered hook will do the job. This is often a good way of using up the gap of a few inches down the side of the washer or fridge. You could also try hanging them on the insides of cupboard doors.

- Wicker baskets can make attractive storage for a variety of items when three or four are placed on a higher shelf. Just be careful that this extra storage space does not encourage you to keep things that you really should be throwing away. It's so easy to just fling something in a basket, out of sight.

- Buy a baking tray organizer. This will keep baking trays, serving platters, Swiss roll tins and trays stacked neatly side by side, readily accessible. An alternative is to screw lengths of plywood to the base of a cupboard to stop trays and so on from falling over when they are stacked side by side.

- Cleaning materials can be stored in a carrying caddy that will keep them altogether as well as allowing you to carry them from room to room. This can also save you money because you only need one set of cleaning materials because you are carrying them around rather than keeping spare sets in each room.

- Try storing your spices on the back of a cupboard door. Plastic-coated wire racks can be found for just this purpose – not only do they free up the space on your worktop usually taken up by a conventional spice rack, they also make it easy to see where everything is. Make sure that you have a thorough clear out of your herbs and spices first – most dried herbs lose their flavour after about a year, while spices are best used up within six months. A good test is to sniff them – if they still smell potent, they should be okay.

> **Top tip**
>
> Use square containers whenever possible – they make better use of space than round ones.

Summary

In this chapter you have:

- Started to understand how your kitchen works for you, and reviewed the different uses to which you might put this hard-working space. You have considered what things you use every day and which, therefore, might justify their space on the work surfaces.
- Learned how to start clearing your work surfaces and how to pare down the remaining items to just what you use on a daily basis – toaster, kettle, bread bin and knife block.
- Learned the importance of categorizing your clutter areas in your kitchen so that you can work on them one at a time. You have also discovered how to conquer the multiplying pile of empty plastic storage boxes and your collection of recipe books.
- Considered plenty of storage ideas for the kitchen.

Action plan

The kitchen is such an important area that it is vital to clear as much clutter from it as possible. Carry out the following tasks and you should be well on the way to a tidy, organized and workable kitchen:

- List all the things that you really can't manage without on your work surfaces. Then throw out all the rubbish that is there, take items away that belong somewhere else, and find new storage spaces for all the other items until you are just left with the items on your list.
- Sort out just one drawer in your kitchen. Set a timer for 30 minutes and go to it. Preferably choose your messiest drawer – the one that you often have difficulty closing – and be ruthless.

- Select just one of your food storage areas – the fridge, freezer, larder or a cupboard – and give it a good clean out. Take everything out and don't put anything back in unless you are sure you need it and will eat it.
- Tackle a problem area. This might be where you keep all those empty plastic storage boxes in a teetering pile with the lids loose that are always trying to escape from the cupboard, or it may be that ever growing pile of supermarket carrier bags. Pare them down and arrange storage.
- Try out one of the storage ideas given in this chapter.

05

bathroom bliss

In this chapter you will learn:
- how to reduce the junk in your bathroom
- ideas for storage in the bathroom
- how to clear out your medicine cabinet.

Your bathroom should be an oasis. It should be somewhere you can relax, perhaps with a long, lazy soak in the bath surrounded by candles. Yet it should also be somewhere that is functional. You need to be able to get your face, body, hair and teeth clean on a regular basis, then get off to work or to deal with the rest of your day. If the bathroom is full of junk – old toiletries and medicines, toppling piles of towels, kids' toys, empty containers, old toothbrushes, make-up items and cleaning materials – it will not fulfil any of the demands you make of it. It will be neither restful nor efficient.

The bathroom is often one of the smallest rooms in the house, so the organization, decluttering and storage in this area must be of the highest order. As bathroom makeovers are extremely expensive, far better to make the most of what you have by thoroughly de-junking the room and bringing in attractive storage.

Top tip

Do not buy any storage items until you have cleared out your clutter. You will not be able to see what you need to buy until you know what you have left to store.

What do you need in a bathroom?

Bathrooms have to work hard because there are many things that must be stored there and your bathroom may also have to serve the needs of several, very different, family members. This results in an enormous variety of things to be stored – and all in a very small space.

Apart from the medicine cabinet – more of that later in the chapter – with its collection of useful remedies, there are all the toiletries we use, towels, toothpaste, and brushes and cleaning materials. If all these items are overstocked and on haphazard display rather than stored neatly, the bathroom will not be able to do either of its jobs – it will be neither a haven nor a functional room. The bathroom may also be where you have to keep the laundry basket for use by the entire family. Some things are essential to allow the space to function while other items could be classified as useful extras or even luxuries. The essentials are:

- current grooming products
- current medicines and remedies
- current bath products
- current personal hygiene products
- clean towels.

Note the word used many times in this list – current. If those four bottles of shampoo in the shower or on the side of the bath are not currently being used, get rid of them. If you tried the home waxing kit once about two years ago and haven't used it since, throw it out. If your teenage children no longer play with the yellow plastic ducks they loved when they were toddlers, remove them from the side of the bath. If your athlete's foot has cleared up, the remedy is no longer current so bin it! When you've done the initial blitz, make this culling of bathroom products part of your cleaning routine. In this way you will be making a more relaxing, efficient room.

In addition to the essentials in your bathroom, you may want to add a few personal touches to create the atmosphere you are after. A word of warning here – don't go overboard. A few carefully chosen items will enhance your bathroom, changing a room with a utilitarian feel into one where you will be happy to go to soak and relax, or that will make you feel ready to start the day when you pay your routine morning visit. Items you might want to include:

- a few candles
- a plant
- bathmats
- a waste bin – preferably covered
- a shower radio
- something to read.

Below are a dozen items that you can throw out straight away. Go into your bathroom armed with a sturdy plastic sack or a box and remove these things. The impact will be immediate and will help you to see what you really need to keep in your bathroom.

- Out-of-date medicines, vitamins and health products. NB: Medicines and tablets should not be put in the bin or flushed away – they should be returned to the pharmacy or doctor's surgery for safe disposal.

- Old tubes of toothpaste.
- Empty cartons from cotton buds.
- Perfume and aftershave that has dust on the box or bottle and is never used.
- Empty bottles of shampoo and conditioner.
- Any gadgets we no longer use – if we ever did use them. This will include manicure kits, electric shavers and depilation gadgets, massage mitts and any other clever but unused items.
- The back scrubbing brush that's lost its handle.
- The piece of pumice stone or face flannel that has started to smell.
- All those free toiletries that you brought back from hotels and which are now gathering dust.
- Toothbrushes that are older than a few months and are showing signs of wear. Keep just one old one in your cleaning kit and ditch the rest.
- All the free sachets of shampoo, face cream and conditioner that you've kept from magazines but never used – they've probably gone off by now.
- The hair removal wax that you tried once – two years ago – but haven't summoned up enough courage to use again.

Now take those bags and boxes to the rubbish bin. Once you've made an impression on your bathroom, it will look better and you can get on with your decluttering task. You will need to apply the general principles of decluttering (refer back to Chapter 1 if you need help here). As always, tackle one area at a time. The bathroom could be divided into zones such as the medicine cabinet, the floor, the laundry basket, the surfaces (window sill, shelves and so on), the shower and the side of the bath (or even in the bath if the children's toys have really taken over!). Go through the task systematically until you are sure that you have removed everything that is useless (this will usually be the bigger pile in the bathroom) and everything that belongs somewhere else in your home. There won't be too many items for selling or sending to charity shops.

When you are confident that everything left in your bathroom belongs there and will be used regularly, you can take on the task of stashing it back in place. For this, you may need to look at some storage solutions.

Storage in the bathroom

The purpose of storage in the bathroom – apart from containing all your items – is to keep the floor clear and the surfaces, such as the window sill, side of the bath and the floor of the shower free of clutter. As we've already seen, the bathroom should be both efficient and relaxing, so storage that works extra hard is essential. The storage options are varied:

- Baskets – see-through baskets can be used for toiletries, while wicker baskets will hide more personal items.
- The airing cupboard – if your airing cupboard is situated in the bathroom, it can be a valuable area for storing clean towels or spare loo rolls, saving the space that a shelf or basket would have taken.
- Bathroom caddies – to go over the bath or on the shower wall. These will keep shower products, shampoos, back scrubbers, sponges and wash cloths handy but in one place. Plastic containers or wire caddies coated in plastic are the best option as simple metal ones are likely to rust.
- Plastic crates for the children's bath toys – make sure you limit the number of toys that can be kept in the bathroom and also that the toys are returned to the crate as soon as bath time is over.
- Pegs – one for each of the family to hang up damp towels. If you're short of wall space, don't forget the back of the door.
- A laundry basket – be absolutely strict in enforcing the rule that no dirty clothes or towels are ever to be dumped on the floor.
- Storage units – shelving units on castors, for instance, can provide a valuable area of extra storage and some are quite compact to fit into the awkward spaces often found in bathrooms.
- Medicine chest – these can serve a double purpose in that many have mirrored doors so, hung in an appropriate place, such as over the sink, they can provide plenty of storage and, often, the only mirror in the room. There is more about decluttering the medicine cabinet in the next section.
- Under the sink – a vanity unit is an invaluable option in a busy bathroom. If you can fit this type of sink into your plans, you will be able to store cleaning materials plus toiletries and personal grooming items out of sight. This will help to keep the bathroom looking clean and tidy, but beware of overloading such a unit or allowing it to become a cluttered space.

figure 7 made-to-measure storage in a bathroom

- Cutlery trays – these can come in handy in the bathroom to store small items such as tweezers, brushes, nail files, cotton buds and shaving tackle.
- Bags – these can be hung on pegs and provide storage for kids' toys, toiletries, spare toilet rolls and so on.
- Made-to-measure storage. If you have a run of space along one wall – even half a metre of space where you can install floor-to-ceiling storage – or awkward shaped spaces under stairs or by airing cupboards, then a competent carpenter will be able to fit cupboards for you that will make the most of the space available. Then, behind closed doors, you will be able to store all your bathroom bits and pieces to ensure that this room looks clean, tidy, efficient and luxurious. A more economical way of providing this sort of storage might be to fit a blind or curtain across an alcove to hide shelves.

With a selection of these storage options to suit your needs, you will soon have a bathroom that works for you. You will be able to limit the things that are placed on window sills and the side of the bath to those few items that you use on a daily basis. Everything else will either have gone from the bathroom or be stored in a more appropriate – and tidy – way.

The medicine cabinet

Old medicines can be dangerous. Have a thorough clear out of any prescribed medicines that are no longer being taken and also the over-the-counter remedies that are out-of-date. It is surprising how time passes and those flu powders you bought will soon be two years old and no longer fit for use. Outdated medicines are potentially dangerous, particularly if you have children or pets in the house. Are you sure that you really need any of the products in your medicine cabinet? Many people don't have any of them – and they're still healthy and happy. You may feel better – and have a healthier outlook – if you don't start every day by opening your cabinet and looking at the clutter.

Start the decluttering of your medicine cabinet by removing every single bottle, tube and packet. Make a decision on each item as you touch it – throw it or keep it. In this area, the decision is simpler than in others because there is no option of giving or selling the item to someone else.

> **Top tip**
>
> Be careful how you dispose of old medicines. You should take tablets and medicines to the pharmacy or doctor's surgery.

Toiletries and towels

The things that you keep in your bathroom must be kept under control to avoid the cluttered look that can develop within only a day or two in such a confined, hard-working space. Here are some hints that will help you to keep it tidy:

- Deal with laundry regularly. If you can only fit a small laundry basket into the space but have lots of laundry, you will need to clear it every couple of days to avoid the overspill that will always make the bathroom look cluttered.
- If laundry causes a major problem in the bathroom, consider whether you can store it somewhere else – maybe a corner of a bedroom – or give everyone a small basket to keep in their own rooms.
- Make sure that everyone hangs up their towels. Wet towels on the floor is not a good look.
- Don't be tempted by every new bathroom product that comes on to the market. If you've already got a bottle of shampoo in the shower, you don't need to try out the new miracle cure for fine hair that's being heavily advertised until you've used up your current bottle.
- Look at the storage ideas above and invest in one or two that will suit you.

Summary

In this chapter you have:

- Learned what really belongs in your bathroom – current products for grooming, for use in the bath, for personal hygiene or treating ailments, and clean towels.
- Learned what does not belong in your bathroom – anything old or out-of-date (medicines, vitamins, toothpaste, perfume), any empty bottles and packaging, anything broken or worn out, anything you've not used in months.
- Discovered some storage solutions for use in your bathroom.
- Been given some tips on keeping clutter under control.

Action plan

- Spend just 30 minutes in your bathroom removing anything not in the list of essentials given at the beginning of this chapter.
- Give the medicine cabinet a thorough clean. Remove everything, wipe out the inside of the cabinet, and do not put anything back in there unless it is currently used by a member of your family. This includes prescribed and over-the-counter medicines; all you have to decide is whether you throw it out or put it back.
- Establish a laundry routine to ensure that your laundry basket is emptied regularly – well before it overflows and causes clutter in the bathroom.

06
reducing paperwork and tidying up your computer

In this chapter you will learn:
- how to reduce your paperwork to manageable proportions
- how to develop new systems to control your paperwork
- how to deal with all those e-mails.

We all heard the declaration that accompanied the proliferation of personal computers, laptops, mobile phones and the powerful computers used in business today – 'The paperless office is on its way'. Have you noticed a decrease in the amount of paperwork in your life? No, neither have I. The paperless society is a myth. If anything, there is more paper in our daily lives now than ever before. The majority of people have a PC in their homes, and who doesn't print out at least some of the work that is produced on it? The art of marketing has developed to such an extent over recent years that we are all inundated with junk mail – the advertisements for credit cards or low-cost loans, books that will change your life, 'free' holidays, supermarket special offers – every single day. The age of consumerism is with us, and it brings with it more and more paper. If you buy a new washing machine, you also get an instruction booklet, a guarantee, a receipt, perhaps a credit card statement and so on. We cannot manage without paper in our lives and so we have to learn to manage it.

Breaking the task into stages

One word of warning – paper is notoriously time-consuming. That is why you need to control it and then keep it within manageable boundaries. It is time-consuming to sort it out, and you must not expect to be able find all the paper, sort it, set up a new filing system and then file all the surviving paper in just one session. To make it easier, break the task down into stages.

There are three steps to conquering the paperwork problems you have:

1 Decide what you need

There are many reasons why you may need to retain paper, and each of these reasons demands that you ask different questions of yourself so that you can deal with the paper. You may be keeping paper:

- To read later – why not read it now? Could you skim through the article, memo or magazine and then throw it away? Will you really read it later? Is it vital that you read it at all?

- Because it just might come in handy – isn't this just insecurity and procrastination? Make a decision now – is it necessary to retain this particular piece of paper or not?
- Because you haven't decided yet what to do with it – again, don't put off the decision. You only really have three options – action it, file it or throw it.
- Because it is vital to your work or to your home – this is a genuine 'keep it' so you must find the right place to put it. See the sections on filing systems below.
- Because there is a legal requirement to keep it – some documents like financial records, contracts, wills, birth and marriage certificates, for instance, come with a legal requirement to retain them, whether for a certain period of time as in the case of tax records or bank statements or forever as in the case of certificates that you will need to produce throughout your life.
- As it will be useful – genuinely useful – in the future. This includes investment details (maybe not the annual updates but at least the receipts for investments you have made), receipts for larger purchases (these often form part of the guarantee so make sure you keep these where you can lay your hands on them should you have a problem with the product) and medical information (while you may want to forget the illness or the operation, you and perhaps your children could find the details useful if there are problems later).
- To give to someone else – so give it to them!
- Because you haven't worked on it yet – this needs to be put into an action file or box. This could include bills still to be paid, projects to be actioned and so on.

2 Get rid of what you don't need

This is where you will weed out all the stuff that is of no use to you and start to sort the things that are still needed. For this, you will need four containers (three bags or boxes plus a wastepaper bin):

1 One box for papers that you can pass on to someone else. Maybe a colleague or other family member will be the best person to deal with some papers such as memos and reports, a bill for something they've bought or something connected with their business or hobbies.

2 One box for things you must keep. It should be obvious which these are so put them into a box for filing. You will carry out this stage when you have set up your new systems (see the following sections).

3 A container for the papers that require some action from you. This is the work that you need to deal with and is what will stay on your desk.

4 Put the papers that you can throw away straight into that wastepaper bin or use a shredder. With the increasing incidence of identity theft, a shredder is, in any case, a useful addition to a home office.

Throughout all this, keep in mind that, as with all sorts of clutter, you can only deal with one piece at a time. You will meet frustration and confusion if you try to deal with too much at once.

3 Develop a filing system for finding what you have kept

We will look at this aspect of your new regime closely in the next section. You need to examine your existing filing systems and develop some new systems that will work for you and help to stop the tide of paperwork returning.

Top tip

Sorting paperwork can be daunting. We all find plenty of excuses not to do it. The best advice is to 'just start'.

Looking at existing filing systems

Does your current filing system work for you and with you – or against you? Does it suit the way you work, the way you run your home and the jobs you have to do? Your filing system should have categories that closely follow the priorities that are present in your work or in your home management. Check out the filing system and ask yourself the following questions:

• Do you actually have a system? Or are all your important papers and files put haphazardly in boxes or in piles on desks, chairs and the floor?

- Can you lay your hands on anything you need within seconds?
- Does your filing system contain duplicate items?
- Are you hanging on to lots of things that you will never need?
- Do you have confidence in your existing system? i.e. do you believe that it works well? If you don't have this confidence, you may find yourself reluctant to file things, and keep them by you on your desk – or in an ever growing pile – so that you 'know where they are'.
- Is it tidy – or does it look cluttered?

Developing filing systems that you will stick with

The only way to make sure that you will stick with your filing system is to develop one that suits you. If you can find the right system, you will use it, maintain it and love it. You will also love the time and frustration it saves you. Of course, the system that suits you will depend to a large extent on what you have to file, but there are some basic rules that you can consider:

- Filing systems don't always have to be organized alphabetically. They can be colour coded, numbered, different categories kept in different cabinets and so on.
- Choose broad categories that fit what you have to file. For work purposes, this might include administration files, accounts files, customer files, etc. At home, you may need files for bills, medical items, insurance, holidays and so on. If you decide to go with an alternative to alphabetized files, you might, for instance, designate the red folders for bills (especially if you usually get plenty of red bills!), blue for medical items and so on. Then, when you need to find a dental appointment card, you will know it is in the blue folder.
- Think about subcategories. To keep with the home filing example, you could divide bills into gas, electricity, telephone and so on, and the medical file could have a folder for each member of your family as well as a general one.

- Subdivide as much as you need. The more subcategories you have, the fewer pieces of paper are kept in each folder and the less time you will spend going through them before you find what you want.
- Make sure that you leave space (and spare coloured files if that is what you've chosen) for new additions. If you get another mobile phone, for example, that might need a folder of its own in the bills category.
- Remember, the file names and categories must mean something to you. Ignore the pre-printed labels that often come with a blank set of files and make your own. If you use the pre-printed label that says 'House' and use that file to store your bills, you may use precious time looking for a file labelled 'Bills' if that's what makes more sense to you.

You will also need a system of storage that works for you. If you are lucky enough to have a room for use solely as a home office, you will be able to develop quite professional systems for your storage. If, however, you need to cram your paperwork into the corner of a room used mainly for another purpose – such as a bedroom, dining room or under the stairs – you will need to be extra creative with your storage solutions. No matter how creative you choose to be, the usual principles will still apply:

- Store like with like. Stack envelopes in order of size. Keep pens, pencils, erasers, sticky tape, scissors and other small items together in a cutlery tray or add plywood dividers to a drawer in your desk. Keep all paper for the printer together – many of us keep a stock of different types of paper and card, photo paper and coloured paper and it should be kept together – perhaps in a lever arch file or box.
- Label as much as you can – then you'll know where to put things back. For example, if you have shelves in a cupboard where you store envelopes, copier paper, blank disks, spare pens, letter headed paper, etc., label the edge of the shelves. This will help to keep your stationery supplies tidy and organized and will save you time scrabbling about in the depths of the stationery cupboard, searching for a new scrap pad.

Junk mail

As we've seen, junk mail is all the paperwork (that you did not request) that comes through your door or into your in-tray on a daily basis. It is usually general in nature – a loan offer that could apply to almost anyone or an 'amazing' special offer for something that many people might be persuaded to buy – and does not normally refer specifically to you. It may, of course, have your name on it as companies who are trying to sell things, whether to the general public or to business contacts, use lists of names and addresses that they may have bought. You need to make a quick decision about whether the contents of junk mail are of any interest to you. Make it a habit not to put this sort of mail down until you have made that all-important decision. Most of this mail will be of no interest to you at all, but don't throw it away without opening it – it just might be something important. Instead, open it, make that decision then take the appropriate action straight away – action it, pass it on, file it or throw it.

If you receive junk mail in such quantities that it becomes a chore to deal with it every day, you should make a serious attempt to reduce the amount you get. The main way you can do this is by becoming part of the Mailing Preference Service. This is easy to register for online www.mpsonline.org.uk and will significantly reduce the amount of junk mail you receive. You can also opt out of receiving unaddressed leaflets delivered by Royal Mail at www.royalmail.com. Incidentally, you can also vastly reduce the number of unsolicited sales calls you receive at home by contacting a similar organization – The Telephone Preference Service. The addresses and telephone numbers for these organizations are included in the 'Taking it further' section at the back of this book. It should be noted that there are some unsolicited calls and mail that you will not be able to prevent. These are the calls from abroad or the ones from organizations that you deal with. For example, your bank or building society is allowed to ring you or send you sales letters to try to sell you additional services – even if you have signed up to both the telephone and mailing preference services.

At this point you should also review your magazine subscriptions. If you don't actively enjoy reading a magazine and look forward to receiving your monthly or weekly copy, then stop subscribing to it. Get taken off the list. In this way you could reduce the piles of paperwork that accumulate and save money at a single stroke.

The idea behind the last couple of suggestions is that you need to stop paper before it gets to you – this is the very best way to control paper clutter.

E-mail

E-mail (electronic mail) is one of the best ways of reducing paperwork both at home and at work. You can keep in touch with friends without getting out the writing pad, envelopes and stamps or you can use e-mails to do away with internal memos or letters to customers.

However, e-mails still need to be controlled. It helps if you view your e-mail in-box just like a real mailbox. If you kept stuffing things into a real mailbox, it would soon be full of junk and things to deal with, and separating 'spam' (junk e-mail) from more interesting and useful mail items will become extremely difficult.

What do you do with those e-mails that you have read but need to keep? One thing you should definitely not do is to print it out (unless the e-mail contains a lot of detail that you need to work on – then print it out but destroy it when you have finished the job). This makes more clutter and more filing for you to do. You can archive old e-mails on a CD for storage – carefully labelled so that you know what you have stored (if you're unsure how to do this, check out the Help menu). Anything else should be deleted as soon as you have read it.

In essence, e-mails demand exactly the same approach as any other sort of mail – get rid of the junk, action it, file it or pass it on. With an overloaded e-mail system, the first step to take is to clear out the dead wood. Spam is the e-mail equivalent of junk mail and needs dealing with in a similar way, i.e. decide immediately if it is of any interest to you and then get rid of it. If you can reduce the amount of unsolicited e-mails that you receive – spam – then you will reduce the clutter in your inbox immediately. Many e-mail services incorporate a spam filter – make sure that yours is set correctly to block any e-mails that you do not want. Alternatively, you can install software to do the job – check out the internet for suppliers. All the e-mails from friends arranging to meet next week (you have put the time and date in your diary, haven't you?) or telling you that little Susie has tonsillitis should be deleted straight away. If you delete them one at a time as soon as you have read or dealt with them, then your e-mails should never get into a cluttered state.

Leave e-mails in your inbox that you have still to reply to or to take some other action on. When you have deleted, forwarded or filed as many as you can, it will be obvious to you what messages you have to work on rather than your inbox being a confusing mass of mixed messages.

Next, create some files for the e-mails that you really need to keep. If you run a business, you may want to set up a file for each of your major customers, for example.

If you want to share the contents of an e-mail with someone else, it is simple to forward it, in its entirety. Then delete it or file it.

Don't forget that you will need to carry out these decluttering tasks not just on your inbox but also on your 'sent items' and your 'deleted items' folders. It is a good idea to set a time every week – perhaps Friday afternoons – to carry out this routine decluttering. This might also be a good time to establish a routine for tidying up, then backing up all the files from your hard drive. More of this in the next section.

Tidying up your computer

Your computer is really a desktop and filing system in one. You will therefore have to create a filing system that works for you, and have regular purges of the files that are no longer needed. The effect of not keeping your computer files tidy and organized is very similar to what happens when you let your physical desk and filing system become cluttered – you will waste time searching for files and pieces of work that are not where they should be, opening all sorts of files to check if they contain the information you want. The consequence of this is obvious – the efficiency with which you work will deteriorate. Just because you cannot actually see the clutter on your computer doesn't mean it's not there or that it doesn't matter. The space on your hard drive is not limitless and you need to use it carefully and keep it organized. Too much useless stuff on your computer will make it sluggish or, even worse, may eventually cause it to crash (then you'll waste even more time trying to retrieve lost files).

The solution to this problem is quite straightforward:

- Create folders that will segregate your various types of files. Perhaps you will have a file for accounts, one for reports, one for letters and so on or you may decide to keep folders by customer or by function. If you have to share your home computer, it can be convenient to create a file for each member of the family who will be using the computer. This way you don't have to go through their downloaded games or school project files while you're searching for that letter you sent to the mortgage company, and they won't need to be anywhere near your files. The way you set up your files and folders is up to you – you are the only one who can decide what will suit you and your way of working.

- Make full use of folders. Remember the decluttering adage of keeping like with like? This applies to your computer too. Keep everything connected with your tax matters in a folder of its own; if you're studying a course, keep your assignments together and so on.

- Name your files creatively. Don't fall into the trap of just dating them or, even worse, numbering them – this will not give you any clue about the contents of the file and, when you're looking for a complaint letter you've written or need a copy of an invoice that your biggest customer hasn't paid, you could open an untold number of badly named files before you find the one you want. The file name should describe what's in the file. You could then, if it suits you, incorporate the date in a file name – just so long as it's obvious what the file contains.

- Back up your files regularly, then delete any files that you are not currently working on. This will reduce the files that you have to sift through and will, if you have deleted large quantities of information (especially graphics), free up space on your computer, helping it to run faster – more time saved. Delete all old files that are out of date or are no longer needed.

- Remember to empty the bin. When you delete files and put them in your recycle bin, they will stay there – taking up space on your hard drive – until you empty it.

- If you use the Internet, you will be storing lots of temporary files that are no longer needed. These are 'Cookies' that websites you have accessed will have deposited on your computer. You can delete them by opening Temporary Internet Files in the Windows folder or, for Mac users, access the Cache folder in the Preferences folder.

- Clear out old programs. If you've lost interest in a hobby or now have the super-duper more up-to-date version of your favourite game, ditch the programs you no longer use. Make sure that you delete the entire program rather than just deleting the desktop short cut or the directory for a program.

Don't forget that you can save digital photographs and graphics files on CDs so that they don't take up valuable space on your computer. A single disk can hold hundreds of photos. Be sure to label the CD carefully so that you will know exactly what is on it. It can be very frustrating to promise someone a copy of a photo from your last holiday and then not to be able to find where you have stored it. With proper labelling, you'll be able to go straight to the right disk and run off a copy of the photo without fuss.

Clearing your desktop

Look at your desk. Is it a beautifully polished object, totally uncluttered, the sign of a tidy mind? Or is it groaning under the weight of teetering piles of assorted papers and files, odd pens, little keepsakes, paperweights, clocks, handy containers for pens and pencils, magazines and books with not a single square centimetre of desk showing through – polished or not? If it is the latter, then you have some work to do. An untidy desk is not necessarily a sign of an untidy mind, but it certainly makes working at it more difficult than it needs to be.

Think seriously about what really needs to be on your desk. When you have finished decluttering it, the only paper you should be left with is the work you are currently dealing with and your diary. You might want to consider ditching the diary too – try using the Outlook software (or similar management tool) on your computer. You will also probably have a computer and a phone. Everything else should have a place of its own. We'll discuss these places further a little later in this chapter.

To start decluttering your desktop, arm yourself with three boxes and a wastepaper bin and then start with your first pile of papers and decide what to do with the first piece of paper in that pile.

There are, at this stage, only four actions that you are considering:

1 Throw it out.
2 File it.
3 Action it.
4 Pass it on.

Do not allow yourself to be sidetracked, just keep picking up the next piece of paper, making your decision and putting the paper in the appropriate pile, box or bin.

Keeping up the good work

Having reduced all your important paperwork, organized and filed, you will want to keep things that way. Do not fall back into the trap of leaving things in piles on your desk or on the floor. We are constantly receiving more and more paperwork and we must decide – on a daily basis – how to deal with it. The most important thing is that we do decide. Remember that definition of clutter as 'postponed decisions' from the Introduction? In no area is that definition more apt than when dealing with paperwork. If we do not decide – as soon as we have opened that bill or that invitation or that junk mail exactly what we are going to do with it (and, of course, do it), then we will soon be on the way to a re-cluttered home. After all your effort, this is certainly not what we want so let's look at a few ways to maintain your new system so that it works as well as it can:

- Avoid the frustration from missing file tabs that have fallen off into the bottom of the filing drawer, leaving you guessing what the file contains, by fixing the tabs securely – a little bit of sticky tape here can work wonders.
- Make sure that you can read the labels you have attached. Invest in a label maker if your handwriting is not as neat as it could be.
- Deal with it straight away. Whatever you receive, make sure that you take the appropriate action without delay. This is the single most important way to keep your paper clutter under control. Put each piece of paperwork that comes into your home in one of four places – your action tray, your file-it tray, your read-it-later tray or the bin (better still, file them, action them, read them or bin them immediately and do away with the trays). Whatever you do, don't be tempted to leave correspondence in a pile to deal with later because later never comes and the pile will grow bigger and bigger. If you don't get into a 'deal with it now' habit, you will soon be back where you started.
- Keep on top of your filing. Set aside half an hour once a week to clear your filing tray and to deal with bill paying and other correspondence.

- Keep things current. Set yourself times when it will suit you best to have a clear out – maybe twice a year in January and July, for example. This is when you can go through your files (and don't forget, they will not be so daunting now that you have got them under control – your aim here is to keep them that way) and remove anything that is no longer needed. For instance, you may have a file containing local information – theatre listings, notification of festivals that you might go to, 'What's on' mailings and so on – and when you go through this in the New Year, you can immediately throw out all those that relate to events that took place in the previous year.
- If you haven't already done so, switch your regular bills to payment by direct debit. This will mean that when bills arrive you can give them a quick check to make sure they're correct and then put them straight into your filing tray. This will save the time you used to spend finding your cheque book, stamps and envelopes, and will also mean that you will never forget to pay a bill.

Summary

In this chapter you have:

- Discovered the four options you have when sorting out paperwork – pass it on, file it, action it or throw it.
- Learned the reasons why you may need to keep some paperwork – to work on (action it), to read later (file it), for legal purposes (file it) or because it will be genuinely useful in the future (file it).
- Decided what you can get rid of – passing some on to colleagues and putting all the rest into the bin.
- Learned how to reduce junk mail and how to deal with the paperwork you receive on a daily basis.
- Got ideas about conquering spam and organizing your e-mail. This involves dealing with it straight away by taking action (replying, forwarding or reading), filing it (in folders on your computer that replicate a conventional filing system) or throwing it away (deleting it).
- Learned how to keep your desktop clear and tidy by decluttering it in the usual way and then keeping only essential items including things that you are currently working on.

- Sorted out your computer by creating a system of folders to keep like with like, giving files names that mean something, backing up your files and emptying the bin regularly, deleting temporary files and clearing out old programs.
- Assessed your existing systems for storing paperwork to make sure that they work for you.
- Developed new systems to keep you organized.
- Been given some tips on how to prevent clutter building up again – good labelling for your files, dealing with mail and work straight away, organizing payment of regular bills, filing frequently and clearing out your files at least twice a year.

Action plan

Even if you don't work from home or have an office to organize and only have household paperwork, you will still have a problem with paperwork if you don't declutter and then develop systems to cope with it as it comes in. Take the following steps to start your paperwork control campaign:

- Take just one area – perhaps your desk or where paperwork gets dumped every day – and examine every piece of paper that is there. Decide now whether it needs action (put it in an action file), should be filed or can be thrown away.
- Set up an action file and a filing tray. You will use these when you have got things organized. Don't forget to provide a bin near your working area too.
- Decide how your new filing system will work so that you will be ready to put it into action as soon as you have cleared out your existing files. Will it be colour coded, how will you label your files?
- Find all your birth, marriage and death certificates plus any other legal documents that you have – wills, financial records and so on – and put them in appropriate files where you can keep them safe but handy.
- Resolve to deal with mail – especially junk mail – on the day it arrives. Do not leave anything unopened or left on a work surface in the kitchen – deal with it straight away.

- Choose two jobs to do on your computer that will help you to keep it organized – you may choose to empty the recycle bin and delete old programs or to set up a filing system and delete all the e-mails that you do not need to keep. Try to choose two tasks that will make a real difference in a short time. Don't get distracted by the contents of the files or e-mails.

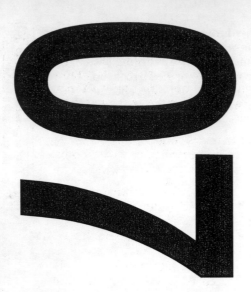

07

children's mess

In this chapter you will learn:
- how to decide whether the children can help to sort out their clutter
- what you should throw out or recycle
- some storage solutions.

It's true, children do grow up quickly. The speed of their development means that they outgrow their clothes and become interested in new hobbies and toys on an almost daily basis. They rapidly acquire bigger feet so their shoes don't last more than a few weeks. They soon move on from playing with their building bricks or teddy bears to demanding the very latest in hi-fi equipment or computer games. This all leads to clutter.

In order to keep children's clutter under control, it is necessary to have a regular programme of decluttering for their rooms. Doing this on a monthly basis would not be too often.

The truth is that most of our children's junk is stuff that we have given them. Left to their own devices, and without the pressures of television advertising (produced by adults, of course) or the material world that we have created, they would play with their chosen toys and wear their favourite clothes until they fell to pieces – then they would throw them out. Junk would not build up. Until we teach them how to collect things, they are not natural clutter bugs. It's not true that children like to live in a mess. They learn junk habits from their parents and the people around them – that includes keeping all sorts of clutter and not keeping rooms tidy. Quite often children are not given the storage solutions they need to be able to keep their belongings in order and so we compound the problem of cluttered children's rooms even further. We need to be aware of what we are teaching children when we buy them yet another computer game with a slightly different set of graphics or another outfit for a doll that already has more clothes than most women. And, given proper storage solutions, there is a much greater chance that a child will clear up their belongings. But should we let them – or even force them to – help to clear out their junk?

The pros and cons of children helping to declutter

Whether or not you have help from your children in decluttering their rooms depends upon many things.

First, there's your personality to take into account. If you will find it fun to work on the project with your kids, then go for it. If, however, you know that you will get irritated by your little 'helper', then you don't have to let them in on the whole project. Perhaps you can select certain parts for them to join in – maybe storing things away at the end or clearing out just one area – and get on with the rest by yourself. Or maybe they could be given another task while you're busy with their junk.

Second, there is the child's personality and age. You will know best whether he or she will be a useful workmate. Consider just how big the problem is and whether it will be a valuable opportunity to teach your child the benefits of a tidy room – and how to get it that way. If you can spare the time to pass on the knowledge you need to be able to clear clutter, you will be doing your child a huge favour. Be aware that you do need to lead by example. Clearing out your child's room should rarely be your first decluttering project. First tackle other areas of the home so that your child can see the aim of the task and will not feel that he or she is being victimized.

Third, will your child be reluctant to let go of some items? Even ones he or she has outgrown or which are broken? If so, then clearing the room while they are not there may be a good idea. You must, of course, explain before you start the reason for the clutter clear out. Discuss the need for space for new things and also the benefits of passing on their old toys to someone else. You may be surprised to find that your child has a true charitable streak in them, and it should be encouraged. You may also find that some children can be persuaded by the argument that a tidy room is one to be proud of. Occasionally, children can be embarrassed to bring friends to play in a room that is a disaster area and where there isn't space to play on the floor because of all the discarded clothes, shoes, bags and toys, but they need help to get to the point where the embarrassment goes and pride takes over. Use whatever ways you can think of to encourage your child to pare their belongings down to a level which you will be able to arrange efficient storage for.

You may have to be very firm about throwing out certain items as your child may want to hang on to some things that are well past their best. Ask them why they want to keep the item and, if they can make a reasonable and convincing case for it to stay, insist that they throw out something else instead. Children will usually understand the concept of 'either this or that', and will feel much better about the process if they have been given some choice in the matter.

Bear in mind that children are more likely to keep their rooms tidy and also to stop their belongings from taking over every other room in the house if they have fun storage in their rooms which gives adequate space for their things. We will look at ways to encourage tidiness in the section on storage solutions.

How you clear out the clutter and how you choose the necessary storage solutions will, to some extent, depend on the age of your child. A baby or toddler, for example, will not need to be able to reach all their clothing in the short term because someone else will help them to get dressed every day, whereas it is essential for a school-age child to be able to reach everything they need. If they can't reach the storage, you can hardly expect them to put everything away. Likewise, a teenager's possessions and demands on a room will be different from those of a small child.

What will you throw out or recycle?

Keeping in mind what your children really like to play with and what size of clothes they now require, you will first need to remove all the items from the area that you're decluttering. Stick to one area at a time – perhaps the wardrobe, the toy box or under the bed – and clear that area thoroughly before moving on to the next project. The usual clutter rules will apply even to kid's stuff, but you will find that the timescales can be shorter. So, if they haven't worn it for six months – maybe because it doesn't fit them any longer – put it in either a recycling pile or a rubbish pile. If they haven't played with the item for six months, ask yourself why. Is it because they have moved on to some other interest or a more up-to-date craze? Or is it because they've forgotten they've got it? Many children have so many belongings that neither they nor their parents know what they have. If that is the case, you will have to decide whether it is worth reminding them of it or whether just to get rid of it. You really must get rid of the following:

- Clothes that don't fit. If they've outgrown their dresses, or their trousers come halfway up their legs, get those things out of the wardrobes and drawers. Most things will have some wear left in them, so pack them up and take them to the charity shop or sell them at a car-boot sale. If the clothes are really in bad condition, put them in the bin or consider recycling options. Some charities can use even damaged clothing. Try not to be tempted to hang on to any clothes because of nostalgia. Haven't you got a photo – or three – of little Johnny in that sailor suit at your sister's wedding? If there are some items that you really cannot bear to part with (and this is usually the parent's problem rather than the child's), then consider making a 'nostalgia box'. This is where you can store your child's first shoes, the photo from the first scan and that really good piece of artwork that they produced on their first day at nursery. Just make sure that you are very disciplined about what you put into your nostalgia box and, of course, store it among your own possessions rather than with your child's. There might also be some items that your child feels sentimental about and you will need to communicate carefully with them about these. Make sure that they realize that not everything can have sentimental value and that they must make choices about what really matters to them.

- Shoes, sandals and wellington boots that your child can no longer wear. Children's feet grow at an alarming rate so decluttering their shoe storage should be done frequently.
- One-off items. For instance, a first communion outfit or a bridesmaid's headdress that will not be worn again – or not by your child anyway.
- Old packaging. Some children may hang on to the bag that their clothing came in or the box for a toy car. Dig them out and ditch them. Some people may advocate saving the original packaging for toys with a view to increasing the item's value in years to come. Unless the toy is to be kept in pristine condition – in the box – and never played with, this argument does not hold water. A battered car in a scruffy box will not appreciate in value in your lifetime.
- The mountain of artwork. Keep only one or two of the very best pieces and ditch the rest. Find a way to display the piece you keep – maybe a corkboard on the wall – so that it does not join a pile of clutter under the bed or in a junk drawer where it will be spoiled and not available for admiring.
- Any duplicates. Nobody needs two Monopoly sets, two pairs of skates or two jigsaws with the same picture, so recycle these and let others have some enjoyment from them.
- Games with bits missing. If the game is unplayable as it is, throw it out.
- Anything – absolutely anything – that has not been used or worn for over 12 months.

Top tip

If you have small children, have a toy swap with your friends. This will help you to restrict the amount of new toys you buy but let your children have a variety of playthings. It can also be a great social occasion!

Another essential part of the decluttering project in children's rooms, as in any other area of your home, is to clear out all the things that do not belong there. This will include, especially with older children, a tray full of dirty glasses, apple cores, dried orange peels and snack wrappings that have been left behind. You must also remove things that belong in other rooms. They may have borrowed clothes or toys or taken items to help with craft projects. Return them to their rightful places.

When the decluttering has been done, a thorough clean of the room will be possible – and essential. You can then start to sort out the storage and ensure that all the belongings are put back where your child can have easy access to them and, just as importantly, in a way that means the room can be kept tidy and organized.

Storage solutions

Storage solutions need to suit the room and the age of the child. For the purposes of clutter and storage, we can split them into two groups – young children and teenagers. The lifestyles and requirements of these two groups can be so different that it is useful to look at them separately.

Young children

Young children will use their rooms for sleeping, dressing and playing. The last two activities are where storage must be properly organized if you are to have a chance of them keeping their rooms tidy. Storage must be at a height to suit them and there must be adequate space allowed for the different types of things that need to be stored in a child's bedroom. Make sure there is space for books and games, clothes and shoes, sports equipment, comics and drawing materials, and hobby items such as skates or construction kits. If they have a crafty hobby, make sure that you give them somewhere not only to store all the paraphernalia but also to display the results of their efforts. This should aim to limit the amount of items to be displayed, encouraging them to select only the best examples of their handiwork.

When you've pared down the junk and organized the storage to suit their remaining belongings, make sure that you take time to explain the usefulness of keeping like with like – all the drawing materials in one place so that they will be able to find them straight away, or shoes put away tidily to avoid hassle in the mornings. The more you can simplify the process of tidying away the toys and other belongings, the more chance you will have of a tidy room.

The following storage ideas may help:

- Stacking boxes can grow with the children – just one or two boxes high for small children and add one or two more as the child grows taller and acquires more toys and games.

- Try toy boxes on wheels. This should encourage them to put things away as they can pull the box to where they are playing, then push it back into place at bedtime. It is a simple task to attach castors to an inexpensive wooden box from a DIY store and then to paint it in a colour to match your child's room.

- Consider investing in made-to-measure storage. Shelves and cupboards that will allow children to store lots of books if they read a lot, or large items of sports equipment if they have them, will be invaluable.

- Use rubbish bins – not just for throwing things away but as a useful way of storing things too. Plastic bins are now available in a range of trendy colours and they can be used to store anything from soft toys to building blocks or shoes.

- Under-bed storage units – especially the sort that look like drawers on wheels – can be useful in kid's bedrooms. Games and clothes, among other things, can be stored here and pulled out easily when needed.

- Use plastic mesh baskets for all the small items – crayons, miniature cars, dolls' clothes and furniture, beads, stickers, hair ribbons and slides, plastic soldiers and CDs.

- A hammock can be useful, slung across a corner of the room and used to store soft toys and other lightweight, little-used items. It will keep the items visible but out of the way.

- Put an extra hanging rail in their wardrobes. Small children, especially boys, rarely need full-length hanging space so an extra rail placed halfway up the wardrobe can double the amount of clothes storage.

- Don't forget to use the backs of doors. Coat pegs can be attached inside cupboard and wardrobe doors for dressing gowns, hats and jackets, sports kit or bags of toys or dirty washing. Try making a few drawstring bags from bright fabrics so that the children can use them to store all sorts of

figure 8 a child's room after decluttering

things and then hang them on pegs. You can also buy – or make – multi-pocketed storage that hangs on walls or the back of doors which is useful for storing lots of bits and pieces.

- In the case of very young children, you can store breakable things on higher shelves, out of reach.

Teenagers

Teenagers will use their rooms not just for sleeping, dressing and relaxing, but may also need space to work too. As they get older, there will be a need for larger surface areas for a desk and a dressing table. Storage needs will change too as they may now have more clothing – and it will certainly be bigger – so full-length hanging space in the wardrobe may now become a necessity. In addition, they will have acquired several items by this time which will demand different storage solutions. This may include a television, DVD player, computer and CD player. All of these bulky items also come with their own extras which provide a storage challenge in the average bedroom. It is at this stage that a thorough decluttering is necessary if you are going to be able to fit all the items a teenager will use into the available space.

All childhood things will have to be ruthlessly pared down. Keep as little as possible and don't let sentimentality on your part or that of your teenager's take over. Bear in mind how much stuff you have to store in a teenager's room and throw out any remaining children's clothes, shoes or toys that you find. Do not let them keep toys such as construction kits, dolls or games merely because they used to play with them 'all the time'. That is in the past and now you need to deal with present storage needs.

Also have a good clearout of current clothes on a regular basis because not only do young teenagers grow out of them at an incredible pace, but they are also more susceptible to fashion changes at this stage.

When you have banished childish things and you are left with more stuff than it seems possible to store, think of each zone of the room separately. You will need to consider:

- The sleeping zone. Many parents try to incorporate a spare single bed in their teenager's room but, unless the room is large, this can be impractical, leaving very little storage space.

In any case, most teenagers will not object to sleeping on the floor in a sleeping bag if they stay over. Don't forget that under the bed can be used for storage too.

- The work zone. Most teenagers have increasing amounts of school and college work and, if you can incorporate a desk area into a teenager's room, it should be well used. A simple table against a wall should suffice with the wall used for storage shelves. Don't forget to leave room for a chair, and add a lamp that will give adequate lighting. It is possible that this area will have to double up as a dressing table and hobby zone, so take these uses into account and add appropriate storage.

- The media zone. Here, custom-made storage is often the best solution as you may have to fit in a combination of items including a television, DVD or video player, computer games console, CD player, radio, plus storage for CDs, DVDs, videos, computer games, board games, books and magazines, and all the disks and books associated with the computer. Collections of CDs and DVDs can be enormous and either customized shelving and storage units or specialized storage items such as boxes or free-standing racks will be essential.

- The dressing zone. Clothes become increasingly important during the teenage years and, even after a severe cull of the things to store, there may still be a demand for a large amount of space. It may be necessary to provide full-length clothes storage, although boys may not have the same need in this area as girls. It is a good idea to provide a full-length mirror too – this can usually be placed on the inside of the wardrobe door. The doors can also be used for storage of small items such as jewellery or shoes if a hanging unit with pockets is attached there. Many of the principles and tips given in the general bedroom chapter will also apply here. In this zone you may need to provide storage for make-up and grooming items; providing organized ways of storing these items at this stage will increase the chances of keeping the room tidy, organized and liveable.

Clutter in the nursery

The clutter that babies can generate is amazing. A new baby in a house gives the signal for everyone you know to buy you gifts or to offload all their own offspring's outgrown clothes, prams, toys and equipment. Some of this will inevitably become junk and, in any event, most babies have too much stuff for the average house to cope with. Of course, there is nothing you can do about the nappies, bottles, pram and high chair, but you can limit the amount of toys and clothes.

Your decluttering plans should start in the months leading up to the birth. If the stuff never makes it into the house, it will never become clutter. As a parent-to-be, be disciplined. Keep reminding yourself that all those cute outfits and toys have to be stored somewhere, and don't buy them. You will find that someone else will treat your baby to that frilly dress or those adorable little bootees and who needs two of any impractical item?

You may also have to try to rein in the grandparents-to-be. They will inevitably want to give their new grandchild the very best possible start in life and they will be convinced that this includes a cradle, a cot, a carrycot, a bouncy chair, a large carriage-built pram, mobiles and wall decorations, a bath set, enough toys for a whole nursery school and zillions of little outfits. Be very firm and let them know what you need for the baby. It can be a good idea to prepare a list of the essentials that you will need and show this to anyone who says they want to buy a gift. As choices are made, you can cross off the items from the list and you will, with luck, avoid ending up with three bath sets but no nappies. You will find that the two spare bath sets are almost impossible to give away – they are gifts after all! – and they will clutter up the nursery for months to come.

At this stage, you can also start to plan the storage you will need. A chest of drawers or armoire is a very useful item in the nursery – maybe you can put it on your list. You will not require too much hanging space at this stage but you will need cupboard and drawer space for nappies and little clothes. Baskets can be used for toiletries. Don't forget to allow space for a changing area and, if you have room, include a comfortable, low chair suitable for use when feeding the baby.

Just in case you are still tempted to buy dozens of soft toys and a variety of outfits for your newborn, try to remember that babies can thrive even if they only possess one teddy bear and are dressed in plain but clean outfits.

Once the initial rush of the birth is over, you will have to keep your anti-clutter guard up when all the notable occasions arise – the christening or naming ceremony (you'll get plenty of mugs, bangles, picture frames, containers for the first tooth), first

Christmas (more toys and clothes than you will know what to do with), first birthday (yet more playthings and outfits), first Easter (egg cups, mugs that contain a chocolate egg, fluffy, yellow chicks to play with) and any number of other feasts and festivals that can be marked by gifts for the baby.

Having decluttered your child's room – whether it is a baby, of school age or a teenager – you will find that you are not only satisfied with the appearance of the room but that there will ultimately be fewer arguments, less nagging, and a greater sense of peace will descend upon your household. It's a task well worth doing.

Summary

In this chapter you have:

- Looked at the pros and cons of your children helping to clear out their own rooms. If you know it will be a bad-tempered experience, do the job on your own. If you want your children to help, your options are making them responsible for the whole task, selecting certain parts for them to join in the effort, or having them do a task for you while you get on with decluttering their room.
- Decided what you will throw out or recycle and learned that the decluttering process needs to be carried out more frequently in children's rooms because they grow out of clothes and shoes quickly, and their interests change, so toys and games soon become unwanted.
- Learned about some storage solutions ideally suited to children's rooms. Storage on wheels will allow them to move their toys to where they want to play with them and might encourage them to tidy toys away. Other ideas include made-to-measure storage for a diverse range of storage needs, stacking boxes, the backs of doors, plastic baskets and under-bed storage.
- Considered the different zones that may need to be created in a child or teenager's room. You will obviously need to provide somewhere to sleep but you may also need a work zone for homework or hobbies, a media zone for entertainment and a dressing zone with plenty of appropriately sized and organized clothes storage.

- Learned how to control the clutter that can accompany a baby even before it is born. Making a list of the essentials should avoid duplicate gifts and help to stop well-meaning friends and family buying things that are not needed for your baby.

Action plan

- Decide whether you want help from your children when decluttering their rooms. Take into account their personalities and yours, and try to find tasks that will motivate them. Be sure to talk to them about why the job is necessary.
- Tackle your child's clothes. Spend an hour creating a pile of clothes that can be passed on to someone else. This should include clothes and shoes that the child has grown out of and items, such as a bridesmaid's outfit, that will never be worn again.
- Tame the artwork and hobbies. Put the best pieces – just one or two – on display in your child's room or bring them into the kitchen so that everyone can see them. Remember to keep this display current and don't just continually add more stuff unless you remove something.
- Choose just one of the storage ideas given in this chapter and use it in your child's room. You might opt for a hammock to get all the soft toys off the bed and the floor and up near the ceiling or you could choose some under-bed storage for games and puzzles.
- Concentrate on one zone in your child's room. Work on your chosen area until you are satisfied that all the clutter has been removed and the remaining items are put back tidily so that the zone is perfectly suited for the purpose.
- If you are having a baby, prepare a list of essentials now, before you receive too many unnecessary gifts.

08

the spare room, loft or cellar

In this chapter you will learn:
- how to tackle major projects like the spare room, loft or cellar
- what really belongs in the spare room and the loft.

The spare room, the loft or attic, and the cellar or basement are often intensely cluttered areas because they fall into the 'out of sight, out of mind' category. Cramming these areas full of junk might seem an easy way to deal with it – but it isn't. We merrily fling bags of clothing, Christmas decorations, old toys, carpet off-cuts, boxes of photographs and old birthday cards, spare bedding, all manner of small electrical items – working or not – ornaments and unwanted gifts, suitcases, picture frames, discarded furniture that is 'too good to throw out' but has no place in our lives, and any amount of assorted rubbish into these areas. Often, we don't give a thought about whether we really want to keep the stuff; we just haven't decided to throw it out yet. They may be out of sight, but all these things will sit there waiting for us to deal with them, and they will find their way back into our minds. We know they are there and we know, every time we go up into the attic or the loft to find something or, more likely, to stow something away, that the place is a mess and that we really will have to sort it out 'one day'. Don't let your magpie tendencies get out of control just because the clutter is hidden away. It is still there.

As a result of the lack of care with which things are stowed away, the spare room, loft and cellar areas are soon in a state of total disarray. This just makes the task of decluttering an even more daunting task than it needs to be.

The aim with these areas should be to clear out things that you no longer need, restore some order into the storage facilities and to resolve to keep the place tidy and organized in the future. Just because these areas are used to store things that are not used every day, it does not mean that we can be haphazard in the way we store things. The storage should still be set up so that things are easily accessible. A tidy loft or cellar is an achievement to be proud of and will demonstrate that you truly have clutter under control in your home. Above all, your aim in decluttering these areas is to finally make all those decisions about your clutter that you have postponed.

In the case of a spare room, you may also need to clear out and organize to an extent that allows you to restore the original purpose of the room – as a guest room.

The spare room

This is the most public of our 'dump it and forget it' areas. If a spare room is so full of junk that we are unable to use it for any other purpose than storage, then we are wasting a room in our home. Sooner or later, you will start to consider moving house to get an extra bedroom so that people can come to stay, but, you know this should not be necessary. Imagine the expense and upheaval of moving. Picture yourself packing up all your belongings, hiring a removal van, putting everything away at the other end. The work of decluttering your spare room will pale into insignificance beside the hassle of moving house.

As usual, you should tackle this job in zones, one at a time, and do not move on to the next zone until you have thoroughly de-junked the one you are working on. If you attempt to do the whole of the spare room at once, you will only become confused and discouraged. There will be a lot of decisions to be made so make sure that you do not try to do too much at once. However, it is of course necessary to go through everything eventually. If you have been ignoring all sorts of junk that is tucked behind chairs, under the bed, on top of the wardrobe or down the side of a set of drawers, then you will have to work your way into the room and tackle even the hidden clutter.

It is best to clear the floor area first so that you will be able to move easily around the room and get into cupboards and drawers that may have been obstructed by clutter. Next you could empty any storage – cupboards, drawers, wardrobes – and sort them out one by one. You could finish the job by clearing the walls of anything that you no longer like or need. Here are a couple of tips for doing a thorough job in the spare room:

- Do not leave loose clutter. Pack it away in boxes and label it so that you do not have to keep rummaging through it, or stow it neatly in the storage that you will be keeping in the room.

- Check whether the items belong somewhere else. If you have stored clothes in the spare room, do you want to move them to your wardrobe? In this way you will have them more readily available to wear. If the answer is no, you do not want to give them wardrobe space, then ask yourself why. It may be time to get them out of your house altogether. This could apply to many things that are stashed away in the spare room. You will need to be very clear about whether the items really do have a place in your life now.

figure 9 a room full of clutter!

Decluttering the spare room can be a very difficult but satisfying task to take on. When you have reduced and recycled, and eliminated any fire hazards or made sure that your belongings are not deteriorating, you will have liberated some valuable storage space in your home. The spare room provides some of the most accessible 'general' storage space – you do not have to go up or down loft or cellar steps to get at it, and the space can be used for all sorts of things that do not have a specified use elsewhere in your home. You will have room for new things and, maybe, a new use for the room.

The most common use of a spare room – apart from storing things – is as a guest room. This will demand, at the very least, a bed (without things stowed on top of it), some empty storage space for guests to hang their clothes and to store an overnight bag and toiletries, a bedside table with reading lamp, and space to move around without tripping over clutter. In short, it needs to be comfortable and uncluttered. This means that, although you can use some of the storage space – in cupboards and so on or under the bed – to stash away the things that don't have a home anywhere else, you cannot allow the room to become overloaded with this stuff. You need to try to create a comfortable, useful room for your guests and for your family.

A spare room can often be used for other purposes in a family – it can become a home office, a study for the children to do their homework or a hobby room. Whatever you choose, think carefully about the storage that you organize and about whether or not you can afford to leave some space for storing what was originally there in the first place. If you decide that the purpose of the room will not allow you to leave some things behind, you will have to find space elsewhere in your home for those items.

The loft, attic or cellar

It is estimated that up to 95 per cent of the things stored in our lofts, attics, cellars and basements will never be used by us again. There are two main reasons for this:

1 We have postponed the decision to throw items out by simply cramming them into a place where we didn't have to think about them.

2 We can't find anything in there anyway!

By doing a thorough job of decluttering these areas, we can address both of these issues. First, we can throw things away. This is the difficult bit so get ready to do some hard work and ask yourself some tough questions:

• Will I ever use this again? Come on, be honest. If it's been there for five years and you'd actually forgotten that you had it, then it's useful life is probably over – for you anyway.

• Is it worth storing? If it is a low value item taking up lots of space, the answer to this is probably 'no'.

- Should I throw it out or give it away? If the item is definitely junk, throw it out straight away – and congratulate yourself on another decision made. If it has some value, decide whether to sell it or give it away. Perhaps you can give it to charity or to someone in your family (but first make sure that they genuinely want it!).

Bag up all the items to be thrown away and take them straight to the bin or the tip. Similarly, pack up all the items that you have decided to give away or sell and remove them from the house as soon as you possibly can. Do not leave the proceeds of your hard work around to lead you into temptation so that some items mysteriously reappear in the loft!

Some of the items that you may wish to keep from the loft or cellar include the following:

- Good sets of china or valuable ornaments. We often store these things away to keep them safe – keeping them for best – but what is the point of that? If you never use or display china and ornaments then you must either throw them out or use them. If they are to your taste, take them out of the loft or cellar, wash them and use them or display them. If they are not, then they don't have a place in your life and you should get them out of your home.

- Things with sentimental value – but be selective here; you probably don't live in a house with enough storage to house every single birthday card you've ever been sent or every photograph you've ever taken, so only keep those with genuine value to you. Only you can judge which those are. Just remember that photographs have only one purpose – to be seen. Why do we keep all the ones that are not perfect? All the blurred ones, those where people's heads have been cut off, the ones with 'red eye' and the ones of landscapes that could be anywhere? Throw them out and try to find a way of displaying a few of your best photos – perhaps in a collage to make the most of a small space with a good selection of memories. If you really can't bear to throw out a well-taken photo of a friend or relative, why not send them the photograph if you think they may appreciate it?

  Also remember that life moves on. Nothing stays the same forever and it may be that things that were important to you when you stashed them away in the loft, no longer hold the same meaning for you. Be truthful with yourself and throw out anything for which the importance, and the pleasure they give you, has faded.

Try making a memories box. Many stationery and homeware stores now sell very pretty boxes (or you could cover a shoe box with attractive wrapping paper) that would suit this purpose, and its size would limit how much stuff you could keep. In this you might put photographs, a piece of your child's artwork, perhaps their first tooth or their first shoe, awards you have won, a cutting from a newspaper and so on.

- Christmas decorations – but, again, be selective. Don't hang on to those dusty, bedraggled tinsel strands, the artificial tree that you haven't used for five years because you now prefer a real one, or the damaged tree ornaments. All these things are junk and should be thrown out straight away along with the dusty packaging that came with them. If you've stored your Christmas items stuffed into old carrier bags and unlabelled boxes for years, and have the problem every December of not being able to lay your hands on all the things you know you have somewhere in the loft, then you need to pare down your collection until you know that all the things you are keeping are ones that will enhance your home at Christmas. Take note of exactly what you have and you can then get the packaging of the good items organized. There are specially designed storage boxes available for glass ball tree ornaments and these work perfectly – but they aren't absolutely necessary. Simply find sufficiently sturdy cartons plus some bubble wrap or plenty of tissue paper and pack all your items into these. Do not store items in plastic carrier bags – strong cardboard boxes will protect decorations far better. The important thing is to seal up the boxes and label them so that you know exactly which decorations are in which boxes, then put them all together in a specific place in the loft or cellar. Your aim is to keep just what you know you will use and love, to protect them in storage, and then to be able to find them easily when you want to decorate your home. Far better to spend your time in December making your home look beautiful than spend hours scrabbling in the loft finding old decorations that you put straight back in the loft because they're not fit to use.

Things that you definitely should throw out of the loft will include:

- Old clothes. If you've been storing bags of clothes in your loft or cellar because they don't fit you or they're not in fashion or you just don't like them any more, get rid of them! Even if you do lose weight and get down to that size again, you won't want to wear old clothes – you'll want (and deserve) new ones. They won't come back into fashion. Sure, mini-skirts have come around a few times but each time they've been slightly different. That's what fashion is all about. And if you simply don't like the clothes, why are you keeping them? Make the decision now – bag them up and get them to the charity shop without delay.

- Things you don't love. If they're up in the loft, then you obviously don't use them regularly so if you don't love them either, they are ideal candidates for the bin. Remember the declutterer's mantra – if it isn't beautiful or useful, throw it out.

- Anything that's broken. Why is it in the loft? If it's there it is out of sight and out of mind so you will never mend it. In fact, you've probably already bought a replacement so get rid of the useless item – now!

- Any hobby equipment that you no longer use. If you've given up keeping tropical fish, get rid of the aquarium along with the pump, the plastic plants and the ornaments for the tank. Items like this could be sold in the small ads in local papers, at car-boot sales or via the Internet.

- Any kitchen equipment that is stored up there. If it is in the loft, you obviously don't use it, so why keep it? This includes food processors that don't fit in with your style of cooking or ice cream, yoghurt and bread makers that you used a few times then couldn't be bothered with. If they don't fit your lifestyle, sell them or give them away.

- Baby clothes. Unless you have definite plans for who will use these in the future – perhaps your family is not yet complete or your daughter is expecting a baby, give them away now. Fashions, even in baby clothes, change rapidly and it is likely that when you drag the box of ten-year-old baby clothes out of the loft, none of the items will be suitable for today's baby. In any case, go through any baby items that you are storing and keep the absolute minimum. Hanging on to absolutely everything doesn't work.

- Any old magazines you may find. If you haven't read them by now, will you ever?

- Unwanted gifts. If they've made it to the loft, the next stop is the charity shop. Again, don't confuse the emotion behind the gift with the gift itself.

- Anything – furniture, ornaments, china, gifts, collections, silverware – that is not to your taste, doesn't fit your life and you know you'll never use.

> **Top tip**
>
> Tackle the attic when the weather isn't too hot – attics are notoriously baking hot in the summer.

The second step is to make an efficient storage area out of your loft or cellar. Don't make the mistake of thinking that any time and money you spend on a storage system for your loft or cellar is wasted because no one sees it. You will see it and you will get the benefit – and the enormous satisfaction – of the improved, efficient storage area.

Start by looking at the types and amounts of things that you have left to store, and tailor your storage to this – allowing a little extra space for the future. The following improvements to your loft area and storage solutions will make life easier:

- Sort out the lighting. If you can't see into the corners of your loft (this is quite common because of the shape of most roof spaces and the angles created by beams and trusses), change the light bulb for a fluorescent strip light or add extra lighting points.
- Make a safe, efficient access with a properly fitted loft ladder.
- If there are uncovered joists in your loft, consider boarding over the whole area. You can buy boards made specially for this purpose quite cheaply at any large DIY store and it is a simple job to do. It will have several benefits. It will stop you accidentally putting your foot through the ceiling of the room below, help to insulate your loft, and provide you with a larger area for storage.
- Put everything that you possibly can into sturdy boxes. Plastic ones are best as cardboard may deteriorate over time. Try not to use plastic bags as they are difficult to store tidily, difficult to label, and will just encourage you to throw more junk in bags on top of them.
- If you have large items that will not fit into boxes, (the Christmas tree, golf clubs, skis) make sure they are kept covered to keep them free of dust. Decorators' plastic sheets are useful for this purpose.
- Label every single box, bag or basket that you put back into the loft. You can use large sticky labels or simply write on the box with a permanent marker pen. It is a good idea to label all sides of the box so that you can see what's in there from wherever you're standing.

- Consider making an index of what is in your loft. This can be kept on a sheet of paper in a clear plastic sleeve attached to the loft access door.

Don't forget the airing cupboard

Does your airing cupboard contain more than just a water heater and a few sheets and towels? Is it full to overflowing with towels that matched your bathroom years ago but since then you've had two changes of colour scheme and yet you've kept the old towels? Do the piles of threadbare sheets teeter on the point of collapse every time you put the newly laundered sheets away?

If you would like to make some space to store other things and to be able to open the door without the fear that a pile of bedding and towels will fall on you, then you need to declutter your airing cupboard. Start by taking everything out and assessing what you have. Be strict with yourself about what you keep. The only towels and bedding that deserve space in your airing cupboard are those that you currently use. If the towels or bedding are the wrong colour for your current schemes, consider dyeing them to give them a new lease of life. If you don't want to do this, give them away because you will never use them. Of course, you should immediately throw out any towels, sheets or pillowcases that are badly stained or threadbare.

With all the space that you have just created, not only can you get organized and tidy but you can also store things that are taking up valuable space elsewhere or are making other areas look cluttered. This could include spare toilet rolls, toiletries, and even the iron and ironing board if you usually do your ironing nearby.

Summary

In this chapter you have:

- Reviewed the possible uses for your newly decluttered spare room – as a guest room, study, hobby room or home office.
- Found out that up to 95 per cent of the things stored in lofts, attics and cellars will never be used again and so there should be plenty of scope for reducing the amount of stuff.

- Discovered the questions you should be asking yourself when you tackle the loft – Will I ever use this again? Is it worth storing? Should I throw it out or give it away?
- Considered the items you might want to keep and the suggestions for storing them.
- Found out the things that you should definitely throw out, including old clothes, kitchen equipment, broken items, baby clothes, equipment for hobbies you no longer pursue, old magazines, unwanted gifts and anything that you don't love.
- Got some tips about organizing the loft or cellar.
- Learned how to clear some space for storage in your airing cupboard by reducing your stock of towels and bedding to those items you currently use.

Action plan

The spare room, loft and cellar provide lots of opportunity for clearing out junk. Use the following tasks to make a good start on these areas:

- Go through any clothes that you currently store in your spare room. If they are out of season, make sure they are stored tidily and are in good condition. If they are just a jumble of clothes, consider moving them back into your wardrobe or taking them to your local charity shop.
- Spend an hour in your loft or cellar and remove any obvious clutter. This could include old clothes, anything broken, old books and magazines. Get them out of the house right away.
- Decide what improvements are necessary to your loft area – consider floorboards, lighting and access – and check out the costs and availability.
- Throw out any stained or threadbare sheets, pillowcases or towels that may be lurking in your airing cupboard.

09

arts and crafts clutter

In this chapter you will learn:
- what sort of clutter is 'crafty clutter'
- how becoming organized will help you to increase your output and your enjoyment.

Creative people – or would-be creative people – may collect all sorts of things that would otherwise be identified as clutter and thrown straight in the bin. You may have the idea that these things will be useful in future craft projects, and sometimes, just sometimes, you are right. However, often the bits and pieces of junk that you hang on to are just that – junk. So, how can you differentiate between useful items and clutter? And when you have decided that you definitely need to keep something, how can you store it without it taking over your home and making it look untidy?

Will you ever use those bows from last year's birthday presents?

If you have a serious crafting habit or think you would like to have one in the future, you need to take a lot of care that your saving doesn't cause problems for you and anyone else who lives with you. Have you still got the cards from your twenty-first birthday – and your fortieth! Do you save lolly sticks thinking that you will make a model cathedral out of them? Do you never throw away old clothes because you might make them into quilts or costumes for a play or into peg bags? Do you save wrapping paper from gifts, thinking that you will iron it and reuse it? Does your button box contain the buttons from every item of clothing you've ever thrown out? Is your garage full of odd bits of wood that might come in handy? If you answered yes to any of these questions, you may have a problem. To help you decide if you need to reform or if you're just being practical, consider:

- If you have ever used any of the 'crafty' bits and pieces that you collect.
- Whether you have some really beautiful pieces that you've made on display in your home? i.e. are you a successful crafter? If not, maybe you should consider curtailing your saving habits for a while and enrolling for a craft class or two.
- Just how many different sorts of crafty clutter you have.
- Whether the clutter is only for you and your family's use? If it isn't – perhaps you're a teacher or a scout master and you're saving these things for group activities – you should see if you can find an area for storage outside your home.

Maybe the classroom or the scout hall has some storage space (if not, have you considered clearing out the junk there as a decluttering project?).

- How many different rooms are affected by the clutter.
- How you are storing your bits and pieces at the moment.
- Whether you have many unfinished craft projects hanging around the house. If you do, finish these before starting any more or collecting the bits and pieces for further projects.

The main thing to remember is not to let your artistic dreams take over. The value in anything is only apparent when you actually use it or it gives you pleasure. If it is stored away and never used, it is worthless. Clutter is still clutter no matter what you call it, and you can sort out the problem of crafty clutter in just the same way as any other type of clutter. There are three basic things to remember:

1 If it isn't beautiful or useful, throw it out.
2 Put like with like.
3 Arrange storage of your pared down belongings in a way that will allow you to get at them easily.

Apart from these standard decluttering principles, there are a few bits of advice that relate specifically to craft items:

- Try to confine all the things that you decide to keep to one area. Find a space in your home that you can use as a hobby area. This could be just a corner of your bedroom or the cupboard under the stairs. Or, if you're lucky, you will be able to use the spare room and have plenty of storage for all your hobby items. Whatever space you can find you will need to arrange it so that everything can be kept in one place.
- Think of ways in which you can reduce your clutter by being more specific about what you save. For instance, don't save the whole shirt just because you think the pretty buttons will come in handy – cut the buttons off and throw away the shirt. Save only the front of the greetings cards that you think you can use for handmade cards. If you keep broken items in the hope that you will be able to use them for spare parts for something connected with a hobby, be realistic about what is possible, then dismantle the object and simply keep the really useful bits. It is surprising how often our good intentions to use spare parts come to nothing, so recognize this.
- Go through your collections of bits and pieces regularly and reject anything that is not perfect or anything that you have

forgotten the reason for which you saved it in the first place. Your aims, hobbies, priorities and tastes will change (and items will get damaged too if the storage method is not perfect) over time – don't assume that your decision to save something is irrevocable.

- Don't be convinced by the argument 'waste not, want not' which often persuades people to keep useless bits and pieces 'just in case'. All those bits and pieces need to be stored, sorted, looked after, moved when you move house and cleaned, so they are already causing waste – a waste of your time and effort.

- If you are convinced that the bits and pieces you have saved can be made into something useful – do something about it. If you don't currently have the expertise to make those Christmas cards into a collage or those odd beads into stunning new jewellery, then enrol in a class and learn how. If you do have the know-how, make time to follow your dreams and give some time to your hobby. If you are now wailing 'But I don't have time!', you may not really be as keen as you thought you were. Think about clearing out even more of your clutter because you probably won't get around to using it.

Decluttering your crafty clutter can be a mammoth project because it involves sorting through lots of bits and pieces and trying to bring order to chaos. Tackle it a little at a time – perhaps clear out all the birthday cards you're keeping in one session and go through all your fabric scraps or wood off-cuts on another occasion. However you decide to tackle it, it will be well worth the effort. Bear in mind that you are banishing clutter to leave the way free for your creativity and enjoyment to flourish.

Types of storage for 'bits and pieces'

There are many different containers you can buy which have been especially designed to hold the wide variety of things that people need for their craft or hobby. Some of these specialist items are very expensive, while others are relatively economical. There are also many household items which can be used for storage of small items and, of course, you can also consider made-to-measure storage units that fit the space available and the items to be stored.

You should aim for a place for everything and – although you may be bored with the idea – everything in its place. Depending on your hobby, and how seriously you take it, you may need to consider any or all of the following storage ideas:

- Sewing baskets. These come under the general heading of specially designed storage and will obviously be ideal to store the small items needed for someone who sews – buttons, cottons, pin and needles, embroidery threads and trimmings. Even if your hobby is not sewing, a sewing basket might be the right storage for you. Take card making, for example; all those little stickers, scissors and decorative bits and pieces would fit perfectly in a sewing basket.

- Fishing tackle boxes or tool boxes. These are similar storage items and can be made from metal or plastic. Fishing tackle boxes in particular contain many small compartments that are well suited to storing small craft supplies.

- Ice cube trays. These are cheap and you may even have a spare one or two around the house in which you could store tiny bits and pieces for a craft such as jewellery making, keeping the various types of item separate and easy to see.

- Cutlery trays. Again these are a useful for keeping different small items separate.

- Plastic bins. These can range in size from a few centimetres in diameter to a meter tall so you could choose the appropriate size to meet your needs. The small bins can line up on a shelf and keep lots of little items separate and handy, while the larger ones might be useful for supplies of fabrics and other bulky items.

- Baskets in plastic or wicker. These have similar uses to the storage bins but can look prettier – choose what suits the space you have.

- Pegboard. This can be useful for getting tools and all sorts of things off the work surface and on to the wall. Simply attach the pegboard to the wall and then use the pegs and hangers supplied to hang things.

- Empty coffee jars or ice cream containers. These are not as attractive as some of the bought storage solutions but they are free. Be careful that you don't save more of them than you actually use for storing your crafty items. If you let this get out of control, you will just have more clutter.

Becoming organized will make you craftier

Many people, especially the very creative types, refuse to consider an orderly approach to their craft because they think it will stifle their creativity. But just the opposite may be true. A bit of structure in the storage of your hobby paraphernalia will free up your mind and let you concentrate on your craft projects. You should aim to create a home for everything you have – hooks for your tools, baskets or bins to hold all your supplies, safe storage for all your paints and glue, and somewhere to keep all the bits and pieces in an organized fashion – so that you can see what you have at a glance. If you can get to this stage, you will find that you come to your next craft session in a much lighter frame of mind. If they are not in a mad jumble of different things, it will no longer be a chore to take your craft supplies out of the cupboard. Never again will you try to complete a project only to find that your session is interrupted by your having to go out to buy a vital item. Instead, you will be able to see what you have and select just the right item from your carefully organized supplies.

Of course, once you have pared down and organized your crafty clutter in this way, you must keep up the good work. After every session, put everything away in its right place and you will find that you return much more frequently to your craft projects because it is a pleasure instead of a chore. A clear space and organized storage will give you the chance of a fresh start.

Summary

In this chapter you have:

- Decided if you need to reform your crafty collecting habits. If you are continually using the bits and pieces that you collect and have got efficient storage organized for your craft projects, maybe you are being practical when you save little decorative items, wrapping paper and so on. But if there is crafty clutter in various rooms in your home and you rarely use any of it, then things need to change.
- Learned how the basic principles of decluttering can be supplemented with crafty clutter guidelines to help you keep this sort of clutter under control.

- Discovered different storage ideas for crafty bits and pieces – from sewing baskets and fishing tackle boxes to cutlery trays and empty coffee jars.
- Found out how getting organized can make you more creative and increase the pleasure you get from your hobby. Like all decluttering exercises, sorting out your crafty clutter will save you time in finding things and will make things easier.

Action plan

- Count the number of places in your home in which you store your crafty clutter. Include your button box, the place where you keep old greetings cards so that you can reuse them to make something else, the box of old clothes you saved to make quilts, all the flower arranging paraphernalia that you keep in the shed, all your oil paints, crayons, glitter and glue and bits of coloured card. Don't forget to count that half-finished sweater or the sets of knitting needles and sewing patterns up in the loft. There should really only be one storage space for all this, so how big a problem do you have?
- Finish just one half-finished craft project. If you don't have anything that you have started but not finished, review the craft projects you have successfully completed. This will give you an idea of how serious your hobby is and will guide you to what you really should be collecting. Dump the rest.
- Choose just one type of crafty clutter – perhaps your pile of old greetings cards or your collection of fabrics – and sort it out. Decide if you really need to keep everything, i.e. will you use it, is it fit for the purpose, are you still keen on that hobby, do you have the skills? Then set up some storage which will allow easy access without cluttering up several areas of your home.

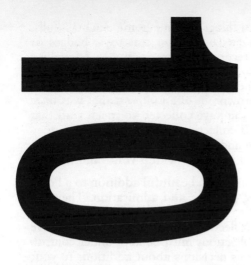

10

collections and treasures

In this chapter you will learn:
- the difference between junk and things you should keep
- how to deal with your collections and treasures
- ideas for displaying your collections and treasures.

Do you have collections of things in your home, such as dolls, china, ornaments, model cars or planes, soft toys, badges or buttons, old books, vinyl records? If they are not loved, valued and cared for, then they could be taking up space in both your home and in your life that could be better used for other things. Maybe you have simply grown out of an interest that was once very important to you or you have collected so much stuff that it is becoming a burden. If collections get out of control, they can take up so much time and space that they start to become the cause of arguments and problems within your family.

Of course, collections can also be a beautiful addition to a home and a source of much joy, pleasure and admiration. They can really show their value when they are well displayed – after all, that is the whole point of collecting, isn't it? Yet, to be a positive influence in your home, collections must be kept under control. You need to make conscious decisions about additions to your collection rather than buying items willy-nilly just because they might fit. You must also take care of a collection to maximize its potential for beauty. A dusty set of model cars, for instance, would not enhance any home. If you find that you have collections of things that you have once loved in the past but they are now languishing in a cupboard, unseen and unloved or are gathering dust and deteriorating on a shelf, making your living room look uncared for, then perhaps that collection is ready to go. If a collection no longer has the same attraction for you that it once had, you should include it in your decluttering programme. Collecting habits are often developed in our childhood and carry on into adulthood. The collections may stay the same (many adults collect toys that were important to them in their childhood, for example) or they may change and develop, but we should not let sentimentality and a yearning for those golden days of childhood lead us into cluttering up our home with things that, in reality, we have already let go of.

Some people have collections of things as an investment. In this case, it is even more important that sentimentality is not allowed to influence decisions about what you buy and what you keep. You must be sure that there is actual – rather than merely hoped for – financial reward in collecting the specific items. You must also keep records about what you have paid for items so that you will know whether, when you sell a piece, you have made the planned profit. Be realistic too about how long you will have to keep items before they increase in value. If you have a large collection of items that you will have to keep for years to show any increase, it might start to cause problems for you before a time for profit taking is reached. How will you store the collection so that it is in a safe place? What if you move house? Will other members of your family value the possessions in the same way you do? Are you spending money on this collection which could be put to better use?

Is it junk?

It's junk if...

- you've lost interest in it
- your collection or 'treasure' is hidden away
- you've forgotten you had it.

It's not junk if...

- you love it
- it is on display and looks attractive
- it is definitely appreciating in value.

Have things got out of hand?

We often start our collections at an early age and, by the time we reach adulthood, we have an accumulation of loosely related items that might not fit into our life anymore but which we carry on collecting, or storing, because 'we've always loved fluffy toys'. The question we should ask is, do we still love it? And if we do, are we collecting in a way that enhances our lives? Or has it become a habit?

If the collection is spread throughout the house, with neglected items left around perhaps sustaining damage over the years, the collection may have run its course. The collecting habit can become quite illogical; we may have an enormous collection of whatever it is we collect and barely room to properly store what we have, but still we buy more and more, cramming the items into every available space. It is at this point that the people we live with may become unhappy (unless, of course, they are just as enthusiastic as we are, which is rare). If your collection is taking over your home, taking up storage space in the wardrobe where your partner would like to store clothes or dominating the dining room so that it is impossible to entertain your friends there, things have gone too far. You will need to rein in your urge to collect more and more things. Here are a couple of ways that you can control your collecting habits:

1 Be more specific. Focus your efforts on finding more unusual items to add to your collection. This will represent a greater challenge than buying indiscriminately, and will limit what you buy.

2 Do your homework. If you're collecting for investment make sure that you know exactly what will appreciate in value and that you treat your collecting more as a business.

Dealing with collections and treasures

Having made the decision to overhaul your collection, there are a number of steps that you will have to take to reach your goal of a viable collection:

1 Find out what you have – sort through your collection and put like with like. You might find that there are some items which you really love and cannot let go of, but that there are other items you do not care about. You will also be able to see where you have duplicated items.

2 Edit the collection – when you can see what you have you will be able to discard any duplicates and any items that are not in good condition. If you have not been able to take care of the collection for some time and it has not been stored properly, it is likely that you will find that many items are damaged. This will not only reduce the resale value but also impair the beauty of the collection. At this point, you must do your level best to be objective. If you are collecting as an investment, do your research and ensure that the items you keep can justify their place in your collection. If, on the other hand, you are collecting items because you like the look of them and they give you pleasure, make sure that you only keep the very best examples of your particular interest.

3 Store it properly – consider custom-built storage solutions. Now that you have pared down your collection, it should fit into a far smaller space, and the storage unit you need for it should be correspondingly smaller and cheaper.

When deciding whether to keep or discard, you can afford to be a little sentimental but you must also be discriminating. This means that you should pick out the best and ditch the rest.

Displaying your collections and treasures

Properly displayed, your collections and treasures can be the finishing touch to your decor – they can make a house a home. They can also make a nicely decorated space a cluttered, untidy looking area. If you have too many treasures in one space, they can overwhelm the room. Moreover, they can become mere dust collectors, and the value to you in terms of attractiveness and resale can be greatly diminished. So, if you have a treasured sepia photo of Uncle Fred and Aunt Minnie on their wedding day in 1920, make sure that it is displayed to its best advantage. Show off your collections and treasures by following these tips:

- Let them shine – don't let them be lost among other pieces on a wall or allow them to be buried on a shelf with other items. If you have a really notable piece – whether a photograph, special commemorative plate or antique vase – give it the space it deserves. If you put lots of different pieces on a wall, the focus is taken away from that one special item.

- Make sure that you put your collection in an appropriate place so that it can be admired. A collection of 1950s style plates, for example, does not really belong in a bedroom. Try to make space for it in your dining room or on a dresser in the kitchen. In this way, not only will your collection be easier to appreciate but it will also not be causing problems and using up valuable space in important areas for storage in other parts of the house.

- Give all your things a turn in the limelight. If you have an extensive collection, displaying it all at once may lead to a very cluttered look. Resolve this problem by displaying just a portion of the collection at a time and storing the other items until you want to change your display. This will ensure that you will be able to enjoy the few items on display at any one time and then have fun making an alternative display from time to time. After a while, you may find that you only ever display certain items – your favourites - and the others remain in storage because you are not as fond of them. Perhaps this is the signal that the time has come to sell some of your things?

- If there is something very small that you want to display in a picture frame, make the surround large. A tiny frame can look a little lost on a wall but a small photograph, a painting, stamp or miniature can look very effective in the middle of a large frame with a complementary mat to surround it.

- If you have a few pieces of art of different sizes to display together, hang them with the centre of each piece at the same level. This will make them easier to view and create a bigger impact.

- Keep valuable items behind glass doors. This will ensure that they are kept free of dust and will protect them from accidental damage. If you put small items on a display shelf, they will frequently have things put on top of them, risking damage and spoiling the display.

- You don't have to match your pictures and ornaments – your treasures – to the colour scheme of your room. This may look too contrived and detract from the impact that a stunning piece of art can make. The aim is to make your treasures stand out, not to make them blend in.

figure 10 an organized collection

If you have decluttered your collections, displayed the ones you want to keep and stored some things away carefully, what will you do with the things you have decided not to keep? Discarded collections and treasures often have to be treated differently to other clutter because they may have a higher value or have a different sales outlet if they are part of a specialized collection.

If you have been collecting specialized items for some time, you will be familiar with where they are bought and sold, and you will probably know where the best prices can be obtained. It will still be necessary for you to do some research to make sure that you have all the information you need to make an informed decision about selling your treasures. The outlets could include specialized magazines where you can advertise your wares, antiques fairs that deal with your type of collection, the Internet, and dealers in your area. Don't forget to take into account your selling expenses – the cost of taking a stand at a fair, packaging and transport costs, advertising costs in a magazine, for example – when you are working out the price you will accept.

Top tip

If you are an avid collector, keep records of where and when you bought something and the price you paid for it. These notes will be invaluable when you come to sell items.

Summary

In this chapter you have:

- Realized that your interests can change and collections can become redundant. If you are neglecting your collections or treasures, you should consider selling them.
- Learned the distinction between junk and something worth keeping. To earn its place in your home and your life, a collection or treasure must be loved, make an attractive display or be appreciating in value.
- Been given some suggestions for controlling your collecting habits – focus on collecting rare items to add to your collections rather than collecting standard things. Make sure you are well informed about the value of the things you are collecting and treat your collection as a business.

- Learned how to deal with collections and treasures – assess, edit and display them or store them properly.
- Got some tips on displaying your treasures – display fewer things and give different things a turn in the limelight, display them in an appropriate place and take care of them.

Action plan

If you're an avid collector, make sure you only collect things that you love and then display them well. Follow some of the advice in this chapter and you will be proud of your collection again, rather than embarrassed at the clutter it has become. Take some action now:

- If you are collecting for profit, assess the value of your collection and write down exactly what you have.
- Ask yourself whether other members of your household are happy with your collecting habits. Then ask them. If you find any resentment or annoyance about your collections, you may need to pare down.
- Follow the three steps in this chapter to deal with your collections and treasures – first, find out what you have; second, discard any duplicates or damaged items so that you are left with the best of your collection; third, arrange proper storage and display.

11

outside disorder

In this chapter you will learn:
- how to declutter your outside space
- ways to keep your car interior organized.

Who does all this stuff belong to?

Garages collect such a wide variety of junk because everybody makes a contribution. Children dump old toys in there, you may have abandoned small electrical items that no longer work, and your partner may have a collection of DIY supplies that are being saved 'just in case'. Similarly, every member of the family may have different aspirations for the use of the garage. One may want to store a bike, while another wants to be able to park their car in there or keep the garden furniture there, and another may need space for workshop projects. You need to decide exactly what your garage will be used for and to organize it accordingly. If you are able to accommodate everyone's needs – to some extent at least – or suggest suitable alternative storage or work space, you are far more likely to be able to stop the dumping of junk there and to keep the place organized.

The same will apply to the shed and the garden. These areas have specific functions which can easily be overwhelmed by junk. If you decide that you want to store garden tools, deckchairs and the barbecue in your garden shed and that you want to be able to relax in your garden, you must tackle these decluttering projects keeping these purposes firmly in mind.

The garage

Most garages are not used to house cars – there isn't space! They are used as an outside junk room. Drive around any residential area on a sunny Sunday when people are out mowing their lawns and you will see just what garages are actually used for. It seems that people have no shame about their garages, perhaps because they don't see them as part of their homes. While they are working in their gardens, they leave the garage doors wide open for all the world to see the mess lurking inside. You'll see a chaotic jumble of bikes, toys, garden furniture and tools, DIY equipment, old plant pots, buckets, discarded furniture items, paintbrushes, ladders, oil and paint cans – and that's only the stuff you can identify. There will be plenty of unidentifiable junk stuffed into bags in corners. Most people use their garages as temporary storage space; they dump things here because they can't decide where they go, and there's the faint hope that they will find the right place for them 'one day'. As we all know, this day never comes and the junk builds up until the garage is full to bursting with assorted clutter. We are back to the definition of clutter as 'postponed decisions' from the Introduction. If you have decided that you are going to declutter your garage, you will have many decisions to make.

The vast majority of garages are in desperate need of a good clear out. Tackling a task of this magnitude demands an organized approach. To make it feel doable, you should break the job down into areas. For instance, tackle the floors one day, the walls the next day and perhaps the workbench area or storage units another day. Try to choose a day when no rain is forecast so that you will be able to drag all your stuff out of the garage and spread it out on the driveway – then you will be able to see exactly what you are dealing with. This makes the job much easier.

Start by getting rid of anything that doesn't belong in the garage. This may be more difficult in the case of garages than with other rooms and areas because it is a less defined space. Most of the things that are stored in a garage have ended up there because they simply don't have a home anywhere else. You will therefore have to think hard about where else you could store some of the items, and then be 'creative' about your storage solutions for the things that will be left in the garage. Ask yourself questions such as, 'When was the last time I used this?' or 'How long has this been here?' If you are in any doubt about your answers, bite the bullet and throw it out.

Consider dealing with the things you find as follows:

- Remove all the rubbish. Bag any old newspapers and packaging immediately. Take this opportunity to throw out all those old college books and papers that have found their way into the garage and you think may come in handy one day – they won't. When you are brave enough to make the decision to throw out all these things you've been saving to read later, you won't miss them – not even for a second – but you will appreciate the space that you have created.
- Deal with big items first. This will give immediate results and will motivate you to keep going. Bikes, pieces of furniture, that old crib or the ancient garden chairs that can be discarded straight away will make space for the stuff you are keeping. The very beginning of a project like clearing out the garage is not the time to start sorting all your screws into their different sizes. Instead place all the jars, boxes and bags of small items to one side and make sorting them a project for another day.

- Throw out any rusty items. If the lid of the paint can is rusted so that you can't open the tin, your decision is made – get rid of it. The same applies to rusted tools, nails or screws.
- Throw out any broken items. If the front wheel of the bicycle is badly bent or that old toaster stopped working 12 months ago, be realistic – you won't ever mend it.
- If something is damaged by time or by water it shouldn't be stored in your garage. Moisture badly affects fabrics, paper and metals and renders them useless. Take any damaged items to the tip.
- Some items will need to be stored in a more suitable place. Garages suffer from extremes of temperature as well as condensation, so be aware of this when deciding where to store things such as out-of-season clothes or old photographs and books.
- Think about the condition of the paints you are storing. If they have been sitting in your garage for years getting cold in winter and hot in summer, they probably will not be of any use to you.
- Reflect on whether the items you are hanging on to belong to another time. This is your chance to get rid of the old cot that your son slept in 15 years ago or the college textbooks that are now out of date or that collection of platform soled shoes. Seize the opportunity and gain some extra space and organization in your garage.
- In the case of supplies you are saving for some future, but as yet undefined, project, decide when you are going to do the job. Perhaps you have a stack of wood off-cuts. If they've already been there for six months and you don't have definite plans to use them within the next six months, shift that pile. The only exception to this might be a particularly expensive piece of mahogany you are saving, but most things kept in this way will be relatively cheap and can be easily replaced if the DIY bug bites in the future.
- Expensive items can be particularly difficult to throw out. You will feel guilty at getting rid of something that cost you a lot, but if it is no longer useful to you – even if it is 'far too good to throw out' – then you must get it out of your life. Try selling it or giving it to charity as this will help to deal with the guilt.
- Don't forget that objects are inanimate – they don't have emotions. The emotions are in your mind. So, your first bicycle that you've kept for 30 years won't be hurt if you

decide to throw it out. You will still have the memory of it and you will also have the space it has been taking up in your garage.

- Keep in mind that your life changes constantly. Your interests and your family's needs will change, and the things you need to keep in your life will change too. If you've moved on, throw it out.

- Try to find room in the shed for any garden tools and supplies.

- Return children's toys to their rooms – especially small toys. The exception to this could be their bikes when you genuinely do not have space in the house for their storage. See the next section for some storage ideas.

- If you come across an item that has real sentimental value, ask yourself if you do indeed love the item. If you do, then you must find a much better place to store it than the garage. If possible, display it somewhere in the house so that you can enjoy it on a daily basis.

- Organize recycling bins if these are taking up space in your garage.

- As always, store like with like, so group all your nails, fuses or tools together.

- Take extra care when disposing of old paint cans, oils, fertilizers and any other products that could be dangerous. Your local council will usually be able to advise you of the best way to dispose of particular products.

Having sorted through each area so that you know exactly what you will have to store in your garage on a permanent basis, you need to devise some storage solutions to make the most of the space you have. This includes the walls and even the ceiling. The aim should be to keep as much stuff off the floor as possible, and to store all your remaining items so that they are easily accessible and you are left with a garage to be proud of. You could splash out on some wildly expensive purpose-built shelving for your newly decluttered garage, but it is also perfectly possible to devise storage solutions for next to no money. This second option is infinitely preferable, although thinking about expensive storage units might just push you into throwing out even more clutter. If you add up the value of the items to be stored and compare this with the price of the unit, you may find that it is just not worth keeping the stuff.

Try these storage ideas:

- Hang it high. Use the walls and the ceiling for storage so that everything is off the floor and out of the way. Lots of accidents are caused by things left lying around in garages, so clear the space. You can use large masonry nails and brackets that can be bought cheaply at DIY stores to hang all manner of objects, from tools to garden furniture. Just make sure you don't use this method for anything too heavy.

- If you are refitting your kitchen or throwing out an old set of drawers, use the old furniture in your garage. Wall mounted cabinets are ideal for storing paints, pesticides and other harmful liquids and powders to keep them out of harm's way.

- Cheap shelving that is perfectly acceptable in a garage can be made from a few bricks and a couple of planks of wood.

- Use pegboard. This will enable you to store all sorts of tools where they will be accessible and organized. A wide variety of pegs and hooks are available. It can be a good idea to draw around each tool so that not only do you know where it belongs, but you are also aware when something is not where it should be. Having a place for everything and everything in its place is one of the secrets of successful decluttering.

- Keep empty coffee jars to store nails and screws. Properly labelled and stored on shelves these will provide ideal storage for small items, and enable you to store like with like. The end result will be that when you urgently need a five amp fuse, you will know exactly where to find one.

- Make up a car cleaning kit. Store the sponge, chamois leather, dusters, shampoo and wax together in the bucket you will use.

Now that you can see the floor of your garage, sweep it and consider sealing it with a couple of coats of floor paint. This will keep the dust down so that your newly organized storage stays spick and span.

By now your garage should be something to be proud of, rather than the shame of the neighbourhood so, on the next sunny Sunday, fling those doors wide with pride!

The shed and the garden

Remember that your outside space starts right outside your back door. Have you left a rusty bicycle there? Or a collection of used plant pots? All this is obviously clutter and you should throw it out before it overwhelms your outside space and hampers access to your garden. If your garden is cluttered with abandoned possessions, not only are you wasting a potentially beautiful and relaxing area of your home, but you could have an accident just waiting to happen. Have you got an old washing machine dumped just outside your back door, a rickety shed in danger of falling down or a tall heap of stuff just waiting to capsize? Are there rusty swings, a rotting see-saw or bicycles with punctures waiting to be repaired? If so, your garden is a dangerous place – especially for children. Sooner or later an accident involving junk will happen.

Also included in the definition of garden junk are dead or dying plants – either in the beds and borders or in unloved tubs and pots. Last year's Christmas tree that still hasn't made it to the council's recycling area might also be cluttering up your outside space.

Remember too that your outside space is likely to be on full view to your neighbours and visitors, and their opinion of you may be affected by what they can see outside your home without you realizing the impression you're making.

If all this doesn't make you want to go racing outside to declutter your garden, then consider a financial drawback of clutter – a messy, uncared-for outside space will undoubtedly affect the value of your property as well as your enjoyment of it.

Choose a fine day to clear out your garden and the shed so that you can spread the shed's contents outside and also make the journeys between the shed, the house and the car (to put the bags of rubbish in the car-boot ready for a trip – or two – to the tip).

Take everything from the shed and lay it out in order to see what you have. The purpose of the shed is to store garden stuff only, so weed out all the things that do not belong there. If you and your family have got into the habit of dumping anything and everything in the shed, this may take a while. Be very strict and remove anything that is not connected with the garden. This might include cans of paint, bicycles, piles of books, Christmas ornaments, sports equipment and children's indoor toys. Try very, very hard to find an alternative storage space for these things.

figure 11 cluttered outside space

Make sure that you make separate piles for all the things you have sorted. You will need four piles:

1 Things that you are going to keep and put back in the shed.
2 Things to be thrown away.
3 Things to keep but to be stored elsewhere.
4 Things to be sold or sent to the charity shop.

Unless you sort everything into separate piles like this, you will end up with a pile of stuff that you will have to sort through again.

When you are sure that everything that is left belongs in the garden shed, plan how you are going to store it in a way that makes sense. This means that anything used frequently – the water hose, rake, spade and gardening gloves – is stored near the door. This is the place where you are most likely to return them to, so make life easy for yourself. Your plan should also include storage down the sides of the shed with a corridor in the middle. This will allow you access to all the shelving and the things stored on them, and it will also allow you to wheel the lawnmower and wheelbarrow in and out with ease.

Try these storage ideas to help you keep the shed organized:

- Use a barrel or umbrella stand for long-handled tools such as a rake, spade and fork. This will stop them from falling over and cluttering the floor of the shed. Alternatively, hang these tools on the walls of the shed using hooks and brackets available from DIY stores. Ladders can also be hung on a shed wall in this way.
- Don't forget the ceiling. Hang small tools and bundles of canes from the roof, freeing up wall, floor and shelf space.
- Gather small tools together in a plastic caddy. These can be obtained quite cheaply from household goods suppliers and come with a carrying handle. You can then grab the whole thing when the gardening bug gets you. Include a trowel and fork, gardening gloves, twine, secateurs, scissors, a dibber (or an old pencil that serves the same purpose), kneepads and any other small items that you use regularly in the garden. You could also use a canvas apron with pockets for this purpose.
- Find the right sized box to store all those seed packets that spread themselves all over the shed floor. This will keep them all in the same place so that you do not buy more than you need simply because you didn't know what you had.

- Use plastic bins to store compost – this will stop it from spilling out of a split plastic bag on to the floor.
- Store all the garden chemicals together – the fertilizer, slug pellets, moss killer, weedkiller and rooting powder – on a shelf. Consider keeping these on the top shelf so that they are out of the way of children and pets. While you're doing this, double-check the contents and throw out anything that is out of date.
- Keep cables off the floor and untangled by using a cable tidy that you can buy from DIY stores.
- Stack plant pots inside each other in order of size.

Top tip

Keep your shed contents hidden from view by hanging some simple curtains – nothing too fancy – so that thieves cannot see what is there.

Your car

How long do you spend in your car every week? Probably several hours or even days! Does it show? Are there newspapers, parking tickets, apple cores, takeaway meal packaging, sweet wrappers, drink cartons and cans, used-up air fresheners, six pens, four torches and three road atlases cluttering up the interior? Is the boot so full of junk that you have to empty it when you're going on holiday because you can't fit in all the luggage? Anywhere that we spend time will become cluttered unless we make moves to keep it under control. Count your car as 'outside space' and de-junk it along with the shed and the garage. Decluttering your car can be done in just the same way as any room in your home. You need to be organized and to set aside some time for the task. Take a plastic sack and get on with it:

- Remove all the rubbish and put it in the sack – all the dried orange peels, apple cores, plum stones, sandwich wrappers, chocolate peanut packets, fizzy drink cans, newspapers and magazines, old mail, parking tickets and receipts, used tissues, notes on scraps of paper and anything unidentifiable that smells.
- Next get rid of anything that doesn't belong there – give the children's toys back to them and return the camera, the books or the kitchen utensils to their rightful places inside the house.

- Now you must pare down the belongings that you carry with you in your car. If you have duplicates of anything – torches, tools, road atlases, dusters, ice scrapers (if you're reading this in June do you even need one of these in the car?) or notepads – take out the extras. CDs seem to breed in any car. You used to have just one or two favourites but now you have at least 20 to choose from. Be ruthless and reduce the number of CDs you carry with you down to a reasonable limit. Consider storing them in a small CD case rather than in the bulky plastic cases they come in. The plastic cases can be kept in your CD storage unit inside the house.

- Clear out the car boot. All you need to carry with you on a regular basis is a small tool kit for emergencies plus your spare wheel – in good repair. Everything else is just excess baggage.

With the inside of your car and boot spick and span, you will want to keep it that way. Here are some tips to help:

- When you're going on a trip, take a small plastic bag with you and put any food rubbish or wrappers straight into it so that you're not tempted to leave the car in a mess when you arrive home. If you travel a lot during the week and regularly eat in the car, you will find it useful to keep a small supply of these bags handy.

- Keep just one disposable cleaning cloth in the car. This will be useful for wiping steamed-up windows, clearing up small spills or wiping mud off the lights. Don't forget to throw the cloth away when it's dirty.

- Be strict with yourself about accessories, gadgets and car stickers – do you really need any of them?

- Keep a rubbish bin in the garage so that it's easy to dispose of your bag of rubbish as soon as you arrive home.

- Keep the boot organized. A bag containing essential tools plus a bottle of water is handy or you could wrap the tools up in an old blanket. This not only keeps tools from rolling around noisily in the boot but it can also be useful if you need to get under the car for a repair.

- Give the inside of the car an occasional treat by vacuuming the floor and seats and wiping the dashboard – cars get dusty too!

Now that you have finished de-junking the car, take a quick look at your keys. Just how many keys are there that you no longer use or even know what they are for? Do you really need to carry around with you the key for the garden shed, the keys for the office where you used to work, or the keys to your parent's house? Is the keyring weighed down with all sorts of little gadgets – a miniature torch (and you don't know if it works or not because you've never used it since you put it on your keyring three years ago), a little set of screwdrivers or a keyring version of the loyalty card for the supermarket you never seem to go to? Time for a bit of serious de-junking:

- Take off all the keys to things and places you no longer own or use and throw them away.
- Take off any keys if you don't know what they open. Keep them for a couple of months then, if they haven't been needed in that time, throw them away.
- Take off all the keys that you don't use on a regular basis. This would include the keys to anyone else's house, the key to the garden shed perhaps or your bicycle lock. Find somewhere safe to store them.
- Take off all the gadgets. Only consider leaving them on the ring if you can honestly say that you find them indispensable.

By now your keyring should be looking much more respectable – and lighter. Aim at perhaps just keeping your car key and your front door key. All the others that you use occasionally can be stored away rather than carried around with you. Decorative key boxes that can be put up on a wall – not too near the front door as that might encourage burglars – are readily available in gift shops and from catalogues.

Caravans

Caravans and motor homes are the very last place in which you should allow clutter to accumulate – there just isn't the space. They are like our homes, with all the different areas but on a much smaller scale. There is the same potential for keeping things that you don't really need but that you still haven't decided to throw out. There is also the danger that a caravan will simply sit in the garden or on the driveway and never go anywhere. They then have the potential to become just more outside space for storage – they become another shed. To avoid this you will need to be very strict with yourself and all members of the family (a rule that absolutely nothing is to be dumped in the caravan) and if you find that you don't use it for regular holidays then there is only one option – sell it – because it is cluttering up your outside space.

Tackle clutter in a caravan in the same way as you did in your home (see Chapters 1–6). Set yourself time targets, sort out one zone at a time, throw out all the junk, move everything that does not belong in there, then sort like with like. When you've done all that, you will be able to devise storage solutions that will allow you to take your holidays in comfort and ease. It will be a pleasure to step into your newly decluttered and organized home from home, and you will be able to truly relax instead of wasting time looking for things or worrying about the state of the kitchen area.

Caravans and motor homes are the ideal places to practise minimalism – in fact, they were designed that way.

Summary

In this chapter you have:

- Discovered that one secret to organized outside spaces is to define the use of the area – garden shed for garden tools etc., garage for a car maybe or a workshop area, garden for relaxing in and your car for travelling in.
- Learned how to make the job of decluttering your garage easier to tackle by splitting it down into different areas – the floor, the walls, the workbench and so on. Then deal with the big items first to produce some immediate, satisfying results and to make some space for the items you need to keep.
- Got some ideas for organizing the storage in your garage including using the ceiling, old kitchen units, cheap shelving, pegboard and empty coffee jars.
- Learned how the state of your garden can affect not only your enjoyment of it but also the value of your property.
- Found some ideas on how to reorganize your shed. After you've got rid of the clutter, keep the floor area clear by utilizing the space on the walls and ceiling with hooks and shelving to keep like with like.
- Found out how to de-junk your car by removing the rubbish and returning anything that doesn't belong in your car back to its rightful home. You can then pare down the rest of the stuff to what you really should be carrying about with you, and do the same for your bunch of keys.
- Tackled the clutter in your caravan – a space designed to be compact and where it is extra important to keep the clutter under control.

Action plan

Your outside space offers huge scope for storage but also enormous opportunities for keeping junk. Improve the look of your garden, garage, shed and car by carrying out the following tasks:

- Throw out all the following items from your garage – anything broken, water damaged or rusty, congealed paints and old newspapers.

- If you haven't already got adequate, organized storage for the tools you keep in your garage, buy some pegboard and hang all those loose tools on it. Then draw around each tool so that you know if it is missing and where to put it back.

- Have a look outside your back door. Any rubbish? If so, remove it.

- Take the decision that your garden shed will just be used to store things for your garden, and remove anything else stored there. Find alternative storage space for these items.

- Sort out just one small area of your shed. Perhaps choose to gather up all the assorted plant pots and – if you really need to keep them all – stack them inside each other, or put your seeds into a box so that you know what you have and can find them straight away.

- Remove all the rubbish from your car. Take a plastic sack and fill it with food packaging, drinks cans, newspapers and magazines, parking tickets, receipts and other scraps of paper.

12

for the bereaved, newly divorced and 'empty nesters'

In this chapter you will learn:
- how to deal with someone's possessions after a death
- how to declutter after a divorce
- how to deal with your children's stuff when they leave home.

Times of change almost always bring with them the impulse or the necessity to declutter. When someone dies, there will always be someone left behind who, despite their feelings, will have to sort out their belongings and make many decisions about what to do with them. Changes in the home such as a house move, splitting up a partnership or marriage, downsizing in old age and children leaving home, will all mean that spaces have to be reorganized and clutter cleared out.

Change is never easy and many of us will resist it for all we're worth, but some things are inevitable, and every one of us will have to deal with bereavement at some point in our lives and with the changes caused by life events. Although it may not seem a pleasant experience at the time, this sort of decluttering can be a cathartic event and allow you to move on in a more optimistic and calm frame of mind. If you can accept that it is a job that has to be done and that it may well make you feel better when it is finished, you may be able to approach it without too much foreboding. Your next task is to decide when you will tackle it.

When should you tackle the job following a bereavement?

Going through the belongings of a departed loved one is never easy. It will take time because you first need to be sure that you are emotionally ready to tackle the job, and the decisions you will have to take – what to get rid of, what to keep – cannot be rushed. If you are sifting through things that mean a lot to you, you will not be able to decide what to do with each item in a matter of seconds. There are therefore two things you should bear in mind before you start:

1 Your emotional state. Some people will want to deal with the things left behind by their loved one as soon as possible. They may find that the experience is cathartic or that it keeps them busy just when they do not want to be sitting idle. Others will be in no fit state to sort things out for a long time after the death. They will be incapable of making the necessary decisions until the rawness of their emotions following the death have faded somewhat. Generally speaking, it is better to do the job as soon as you feel able.

2 It is vital to allow sufficient time for the task. Give yourself time to make the decisions about letting things go at your

own pace. Remember to split the job into manageable chunks. Perhaps you could tackle the deceased person's clothing one day, their paperwork another day and their memorabilia on another occasion.

Of course, it may be that you do not have much choice about when you do some of the sorting out. If you need to find important documents for legal purposes, you will need to deal with the deceased's paperwork soon after the death. Or you may need to empty a house to get it ready for sale or to clear out the room in a nursing home straight away. In this case, unless you feel up to the task immediately, you could simply remove, pack up and store all the belongings to be dealt with at a later date. However, it is important for your own peace of mind and also for practical purposes that you do not keep putting off the task. The decluttering process can help you to come to terms with the loss.

The timing of the task may also be affected by the legal process. If there is any doubt at all about who all the items belong to in law, you will need to consult a solicitor to ensure that the terms of the deceased's will are adhered to.

Top tip

If a close friend or relative becomes ill and has to go into a nursing home, remember that you may need power of attorney in order to be able to deal with their home and belongings. Consult a solicitor about this.

Dealing with feelings

Whether you like your loved one's possessions or not, it can be difficult to make all the decisions about keeping them or giving them away. It can be useful to have plenty of help to complete this task, and this may assist you in dealing with your feelings. It is also a good idea to discuss your approach to the task with others who are involved. You should make clear your views on the possessions you are sorting out so that everyone understands what is important for you. There will be things that you will wish to keep and you cannot expect members of your family to be mind-readers. You will often find that everyone has different ideas about what is important for them to keep because everyone will have had a different relationship with the deceased and will want to keep different mementoes. If you can have an open and loving conversation about the possessions – perhaps reminiscing about your loved one along the way – it will help you emotionally and avoid misunderstandings as you go about this difficult task.

Apart from the sadness that is inevitable as we go through a departed loved one's possessions, we may also feel anger at being left behind, disbelief that they have gone and guilt at throwing things out. All these feelings are normal and may be different for each person, just as the process of bereavement and grieving is different for every individual. The solution is to acknowledge the feelings, take your time and deal with just one area at a time until the job is done. By the time the belongings have been dealt with, you will undoubtedly feel better able to cope.

One way of dealing with guilty feelings at letting go of your loved one's possessions is to select a charity that would have meant something to them during their lifetime and to resolve to give that charity the maximum benefit from the things left behind.

To lessen these difficult feelings and to ease yourself into the mammoth job of clearing out an entire house, start with the less personal rooms – the bathroom or kitchen would be ideal – so that you are not immediately bombarded with feelings brought on by handling intensely personal items such as clothing, photographs or memorabilia.

One last thing to remember is that when you are throwing out any items left behind, you are not throwing out the person or the memories. Your memories of the good times with your loved one will remain regardless of what you do with their material possessions.

What should you keep?

The question you need to ask about every single possession left behind by a loved one is 'Does this have a place in my life?' So, for example, if the item in question is a large, dark wood Welsh dresser and you live in a small house with a tiny fully fitted kitchen, then the answer must be no. You will have to either give it away or sell it. Try not to keep things for other people. If you want to give something away, first make sure that the recipient really wants it, and get it to them without delay. If they don't want it, let the item go. If you feel that you really must keep an item for your children, try to find a place to store it where it will be protected and where it will not be in your way. The loft or cellar – if they are dry and spacious – are good options.

It is advisable to hang on to legal documentation – birth, marriage and death certificates, the will, the deeds to a house (until it is sold, of course) and insurance documents. There are also some items of paperwork that need to be returned to various organizations. This includes the following, which should be sent with a note of explanation and the date of death:

- Any payment order books or uncashed cheques to the social security office (or other office that issued the payment). This includes any child benefit book for a child who has died. It is advisable to keep a note of the details, including reference numbers.
- The deceased's passport to the relevant passport agency.
- The deceased's driving licence to the Driver and Vehicle Licensing Agency (or equivalent organization outside the UK).
- Any season tickets – there may be a refund due.
- Registration documents for a car so that change of ownership can be recorded.
- Lastly, don't forget to return library books.

If you suspect that there are some high-value items mixed among the usual belongings, it is worth asking an expert to do a valuation. When you know the value of things, you can make informed decisions. Don't feel guilty about selling high-value items; your relative or friend has left them behind for you to do as you wish with them. Unless that antique chair goes perfectly with your other furniture, don't be tempted to keep it just because your aunt loved it. It is certain that it was not her intention, in leaving it to you, to clutter up your home.

If, when you have finished decluttering your departed loved one's possessions, you are left with just a very few well loved pieces that will enhance your life, you can feel satisfied with a job well done. If you have also sold some items, you could buy yourself something beautiful that genuinely fits into your home and will be a memorial to the deceased.

For the newly divorced

The time when a marriage or partnership breaks down can be a time of upheaval and it can feel a bit like a bereavement as the death of the relationship is mourned. There will usually be a house move involved for one of the partners so some decluttering will be necessary.

The principles of decluttering remain the same and a lot of the advice in this book will be applicable here but you will need to choose the time carefully when you carry out the task as this will generally be an upsetting time. You will also need to be sensitive to the feelings of all those involved – yourself, your partner and children if you have them – as they can easily be distressed if they perceive that you are getting rid of everything connected with their absent parent.

Before you start this task, make sure that you have consulted with your partner. Throwing out treasured possessions will not make a difficult and touchy situation any easier. If you can gain the cooperation of the partner who has left, the ideal situation would be to pack up anything that they have left behind and have them collect it without you having to go through it all.

When the children leave home

Children leaving home – going off to university, setting up on their own or perhaps getting married – often signals a major shift in the parents' relationship and in the way that the home is used. Some people find this a very difficult period, hanging on to their children's belongings and refusing to change their living space. Life does not finish when children leave home, it merely changes and it is best to look upon this time positively and as an opportunity to create a new and useful area in your home. Start living your life for you and your partner rather than basing it around the children. Becoming 'empty nesters' can be the start of a whole new phase in your life.

It is important not to leave your children's bedrooms as they were – like a shrine to your offspring's childhood fads and fancies. These are things that do not belong in your home any longer. You can get rid of the pop star posters from the walls, the Barbie wallpaper that has somehow remained in your daughter's bedroom despite her not having played with a doll for over ten years, the collection of football memorabilia, the pink ruffled bedspread, or the black and red colour scheme that your son insisted on. Just think of all the possible uses to which this newly vacated space in your home could be put – you could create a home office or gym, or a lounging space to relax in away from the television and the hustle and bustle of the house. If you've always complained that you don't have the space for a crafty hobby, this is your chance. Kit out the room as a sewing room or with storage to keep all your crafty bits and pieces organized and ready for action. Alternatively, you could simply create a guest bedroom to be proud of, where your guests – including your grown-up children – can come and stay in total comfort rather than having to squeeze in among the remnants of your son or daughter's childhood.

First, you need to clear out the clutter. Clearing out junk is a good way to make change positive and to pave the way for a new life. You can reinvent the children's rooms and, in the process, find a new lease of life for yourself and your home. Of course, clearing clutter can be life changing. It might be just the thing you need to do to let go of your children and see clearly that this is an opportunity for a new start. It could help you to see the possibilities that the extra space and time can bring. Don't hang on to the past, get busy creating something new for the future.

One of the first problems to be dealt with is that of belongings left behind. Many children will take the easy option when they fly the nest and will leave things for their parents to deal with or store. It is easier to move out of the home, taking with them just the essentials – clothes, computer, bed and their CD collection (or worse still, just the current favourite CDs) – than to sort out their belongings, discarding what is no longer required and taking with them the non-essential bits and pieces that are still a part of their life. They will casually say, 'Oh, just throw it all out' when asked about the mounds of things left behind, but their parents know very well that it is impossible to do that and will eventually have to sort through the belongings. The thing to do is to make your offspring accept their responsibilities and ask them to at least help with the clutter clearing. If that is impossible, give them adequate warning that the decluttering and transformation of their old room is going to take place. Let them know that if things that they treasure are not collected by a certain date, they will be thrown out. If this doesn't work, you will have to assume that there is nothing there that they wish to keep and that you can get on with deciding what you wish to keep for yourself.

Follow the usual decluttering principles of seeing what you've got to deal with, removing what doesn't belong in the area you're decluttering (in this case it may be almost everything!) and

figure 12 an example of what can be done with a spare room

deciding what to do with things that you can let go (see Chapters 1–6).

When you've done a thorough job of decluttering your child's old room, there probably won't be very much that you will need to find space to store. It is more likely that you will be bringing new things into the cleared and converted space, and the storage solutions you need will depend on the new use you have decided upon. Even if you are going to create a guest bedroom, you should try to include as much storage as possible. In this way, the room can be kept tidy and ready for any unexpected guests. Leave a drawer empty and some wardrobe space in which guests can store their belongings while they are with you, and also provide yourself with some extra storage.

If you've decided that you can make something different out of your child's room, you can take your pick of the multitude of storage options to suit your purpose. Existing storage – such as a wardrobe, chest of drawers and shelving – can be utilized for all sorts of storage needs. For example, extra shelves can be put inside a wardrobe to reduce the hanging space but increase the horizontal space which is useful for storing baskets of craft items.

> **Top tip**
>
> Make sure that your offspring take their things with them when
> they go. If they are old enough to leave home, they're old enough
> to take responsibility for their belongings.

Don't stop at clearing out the children's rooms. Take a tour of
your home looking for things that you would classify as
belonging to the children. Just look at some of the things that
may have been left behind with no use to you in your new,
independent life, cluttering up your home:

- Pizza menus. If only the children ordered pizza takeaways,
  you can throw out any menus that are still lingering.
- Computer games and consoles in the living room. Give them
  back.
- Shoes and jackets still in the hall cupboard.
- Their favourite mugs – collected at the latest gig or festival
  they went to – in the kitchen.
- CDs and DVDs in the living room, that you would never
  dream of playing.
- Their books on the bookshelves in your study.
- All their school reports stored in your household paperwork.
  Pare them down (or throw them out) and store them in a less
  prominent place if you really want to keep one or two
  examples of their genius.
- On the shelves or sideboard you may find trophies that they
  won for sports or dancing. Check if your offspring still want
  them (and pass them on if they do) before you throw them out.
- Check whether you are storing any clothes – a bridesmaid
  dress or their one good suit, for example – in your wardrobes.
- Schoolwork and books left in the dining room.

Another scenario might be if your children leave home to go to
university. In this case, they will want to retain their room in
your home for use during the long summer and Christmas
breaks. You will still need to clear out their belongings so that
they do not clutter up your home even when the student is away,
but rather than changing the use of their room, you could
simply streamline the possessions so that they can be contained.
This is an ideal time for a decluttering session in both the
student's room and the rest of the home.

When you move house

If you have successfully decluttered your home and have kept junk to a minimum, moving home will be far less stressful. However, a house move is more often a catalyst for decluttering. As soon as you get a moving date and start to assess how many boxes you will need, the realization hits you that you have way too much stuff. Moving offers the perfect opportunity to de-junk. Nevertheless, it may not be only a chance to get rid of a few things that you no longer need, it may be a necessity. Think about the costs involved in a house move; moving junk costs just as much as moving essential items.

As far in advance of your move as possible – as soon as you put up the For Sale sign – start the decluttering process. There are many things which can be packed away long before the move. This could include the contents of your loft or cellar, garden tools if it is winter, collections and treasures, your 'best' glassware and dinner service if you don't use them very often, and Christmas decorations if you will not be spending another Christmas in this home. As you pack all these things away, edit them. Ask yourself whether you really want this item in your new home. If you do, pack it, if you don't, find a way of disposing of it before the move.

Nearer the day of the move you will have to, at some point, pack everything that you are taking to your new place. Making sure that you only take what you love and will use is the key. As you pack, you can still make decisions about what you take with you. When you're packing up your kitchen stuff, for example, you can still reject that grimy wooden chopping board. Ask yourself if you really want it at your new home and also if you want to pay to move it. Pack as much as you can in boxes; they will protect your things and are an efficient way of shifting all sorts of items because they are sturdy and stackable.

Top tip

If you run out of time, throw all the last few bits and pieces that you haven't managed to sort into a box and label it 'Clutter'. Then don't open it when you get to your new home until you are ready to deal with it. If it remains unopened for more than a few weeks, you can assume you don't need the box contents and can throw it out, unopened.

Good decluttering and packing will make the move go much more quickly and will make the transition painless. Of course, if you are leaving the packing to your removal company, then you will not be able to take advantage of the packing period to do your decluttering and will have to tackle it when things are unpacked in your new home. However, it will still pay dividends if you can do some preparatory decluttering before the packers arrive. This will ensure that you are not paying for the things that you do not want or need to be professionally packed.

Another situation involving a house move is when two previously single people combine their households and move in together. This can result in a need for many decisions to be made about what to keep and what to let go because there will inevitably be some duplication of possessions from the two households. If you have two irons, two kettles, two sets of cutlery and so on, choose the best and ditch the rest. Don't be tempted to keep spares as you will no doubt want, when finances allow, to buy things for the home together rather than use older items. This will be a source of enjoyment, so prepare yourself now by selling or throwing out any duplicated items.

When you downsize

People move to smaller homes for a variety of reasons – perhaps financial, because the children have left home or because, as you get older, a big property becomes difficult to manage. Whatever the reason, if you are going to be living in a smaller space, decluttering before you move becomes essential.

Although a downsizing move will trigger a decluttering project that can be dealt with like any other, there are several things that must be taken into account which will make the process easier and more suited to your circumstances:

- What rooms or space do you have now which you are not going to have in your new home? Maybe you will have fewer bedrooms or a much smaller kitchen, so you will need to tailor your decluttering so that you pare down your belongings in that area, and make decisions as to where things from the current bedrooms or kitchen will be stored.
- How will you use the new home? Will there, for example, be lifestyle changes that accompany the move? Maybe you will no longer be working from home so you can get rid of the filing cabinets or desk. Perhaps you will no longer have the space for a guest bedroom and you will need to throw out the

spare bed and think of another solution – such as a sofa bed in the living room.

- Think of dual-purpose storage and furniture. With less space to live in, the things you have need to work harder for you. The right dressing table, for example, could also double up as a desk if you need to keep a small office space in your bedroom. Storage units for living areas can be built so that they house your collections of CDs, books and china (among other things) interspersed with decorative items such as plants or vases, giving you practical storage combined with display areas. These could also be used as room dividers if the kitchen is visible, for example, from the living space.
- Before you move, cull all your non-essential possessions such as ornaments and pictures. Acknowledge that your new life will not have room for all the bits and pieces that you may have collected over the years and resolve to get them down to a reasonable level.

What will you do with all that stuff?

Decluttering because of major life changes invariably produces large amounts of things that have to be disposed of. Much of it will consist of perfectly good items for which you can find a good home elsewhere. Various options for giving away or selling useful items have been referred to at various points in this book but it is worth recapping here:

- Sell good items on the Internet. Ebay (www.ebay.co.uk or www.ebay.com) is the best-known site and is relatively simple to master. Make sure that you don't even look at what's for sale on there – your aim is to sell your unwanted stuff, not to accumulate more clutter!
- Sell your stuff at a car-boot sale. Again just sell, don't buy.
- Sell some items through the small ads in your local paper.
- If you have some really valuable items – antiques especially – consult a specialist who may want to buy your items.
- Books can be sold on Amazon (amazon.co.uk or amazon.com).
- Give it away to friends and relatives – but first make sure that they genuinely want to take the item from you, don't pass on your problem. This especially applies to family heirlooms – give others the chance to keep something that they treasure by all means but do not force it on them.
- Give it away to strangers. Leave it in a heap at the bottom of your driveway or by the garden gate with a large notice

saying, 'Free to a good home. Unwanted stuff – please help yourself'. It will magically disappear!

- Give it to charity. Most charity shops will gladly take a variety of stuff off your hands – clothes, shoes, ornaments, books, cameras, jewellery, toys, curtains, towels, bedding, etc. Make sure all of it is clean and in working order.
- Check out charities that may welcome particular items such as furniture, spectacles or mobile phones.
- Take it to the tip. Bag up things that will be of no use to you or to anyone else and take them to the waste disposal site as soon as possible – before you are tempted to change your mind.
- Shred, burn or recycle old paperwork depending on its confidentiality.
- Organize it. If you've decided to keep something then you must make sure that it is stored safely or displayed for all to see and enjoy.

Summary

In this chapter you have:

- Learned how to deal with possessions – yours and other people's – during periods of change such as bereavement, when children leave home or when moving house.
- Looked at the best time to sort out belongings after a death. There were two main things to consider – your emotional state and the time that this task will take.
- Learned about the variety of feelings you will have during this period – sadness, guilt, anger, disbelief – and how to make sure that they do not overwhelm you, by taking your time over the task and by acknowledging your feelings.
- Considered what you should keep after a bereavement – legal paperwork, for example – and got some advice about passing things on or storing items.
- Learned how to see the 'empty nest' after children leave home as an opportunity to get your home back rather than as the end of an era. Your child's decluttered room could become a guest bedroom to be proud of, a hobby room or home office. You choose.
- Discovered how much less stressful a house move will be if you have successfully decluttered before the move. It will also cost less if you are not moving junk that is no longer required.
- Considered the changes that will have to take place if you move to a smaller home, i.e. different ways of using the home

if is appreciably smaller or if the move accompanies major changes in your lifestyle.

- Learned what options there are for dealing with the stuff after you have decluttered – selling it in various ways, giving it away to friends or to charity, taking it to the tip, destroying it or, if you're keeping it, getting it organized and stored efficiently.

Action plan

At times of change there is often a need for much decluttering and decision making. Make the whole thing easier by completing the following tasks according to the change of situation you are facing:

- If you are recently bereaved but feel ready to start decluttering, commit yourself to a date when you will start to sort out the belongings left behind and decide whether you will enlist someone's help with the task. In the run up to the date you have set, you could make some plans – which room or type of possessions will you start with? Remember that you will find it easier if you start with the less personal items. If you have some idea of the amount and type of things you will have to sort, plan what you will do with the things you do not wish to keep, perhaps making enquiries about council facilities, charity requirements and so on.

- If you are an 'empty nester', decide what use you will put your child's room to and make preparations – perhaps buying new storage items or bedding for a guest room. Now start the decluttering project. Contact your son or daughter to see if there is anything they wish to keep of the items they have left behind, then go into the room and assess the task.

- If you are moving house, start the decluttering process now. Choose just one area – maybe the loft, cellar or garage – and do a thorough decluttering job referring back to the appropriate chapter and following the basic principles of decluttering.

- If you're moving to a smaller home, sit down and plan your project. Think about what space will be available to you and how you will use your new home. Take a complete tour of your existing home and note down where your non-essential items are.

- Look through the list of suggestions about what you can do with all the things you have (see page 160) and plan which ones appeal to you and are appropriate to your situation.

13

danger areas

In this chapter you will learn:
- the excuses we make not to declutter
- places to avoid
- how to deal with guilty feelings about gift clutter.

How clutter creeps up on you

One definition of clutter is 'postponed decisions'. This means that, in its most basic form, most clutter is simply junk that you haven't yet decided to get rid of. The process of decluttering primarily consists of making those decisions.

How much clutter you have depends, in part, on how long and how often you have been putting off making decisions. Unfortunately, we are frequently unaware that those decisions need to be made and then clutter creeps up on us. We are soon surrounded by the results of all those postponed decisions – the piles of paper that we haven't dealt with, the clothes that no longer fit us, the unwanted gifts, the kitchen utensils that haven't been used in years or the broken appliances that we thought would get fixed 'one day'. Over the years, we cram more and more clothes into our wardrobe alongside the things that we no longer wear or put unwanted gifts in a cupboard and try to forget them. It doesn't work. The wardrobe will be overflowing and even the clothes that you do wear will come out looking creased and uncared for, and the gifts will always be there – in the cupboard and in the back of our minds. They will be taking up space that we could free up and they will be making us feel guilty even if we have hidden them away.

If you have lots of drawers, cupboards and shelves in your home that contain a collection of mixed-up, unlike items that represent lots of postponed decisions, then you haven't yet decided where these items really belong. They don't belong together, that is obvious, but where do they belong? It may be that very few of the items in such places have to be thrown away but, in the decluttering process, you will make the decisions and create the storage and systems that will enable you to live a clutter-free life.

Clutter increases, and increases, in direct proportion to the amount of time that we continue to ignore it. Therefore, in order to get rid of junk and to make room in our lives for personal development and joy, we must tackle the problem of those postponed decisions.

Where did the clutter come from?

Clutter is coming into our homes continually and, unless we have routines set in place to move it out of our homes, it will soon overwhelm us. It will fill every available space, make a mess of our drawers, cupboards, shelves and surfaces. The frustration, wasted time and money and the sheer mess that it causes will begin to affect our state of mind. It is at this point – and maybe you are at this point if you have bought this book – that a regular programme of action is needed.

One of the main culprits is materialism. In the war years, when utilitarianism held sway and people had to 'make do and mend', I'm willing to bet that nowhere near as many homes suffered the effects of too much stuff as they do today. Indeed, the tendency to hang on to things 'just in case' and the need to buy more and more things to satisfy ourselves probably have their roots in the war years and just after, and are a direct reaction to the circumstances then. From the 1950s onwards, the consumer society has gone from strength to strength and almost all of us have homes full of stuff.

So, where does junk come from? The easy answer, of course, is almost everywhere. It comes from the shops and the car-boot sales that we visit on a regular basis, from the tempting catalogues that drop through our letter boxes every week and from the shopping that, these days, we can do with so much ease on the Internet. It comes from the companies who want to sell us all sorts of products such as insurance policies, new credit cards and holidays. It comes from the other people in our lives in the form of gifts, inherited furniture and books passed on. In fact, often our clutter was once someone else's clutter. The sources of clutter are varied and they are all around us.

It is vital to be aware of all the particular sources of clutter in our own lives so that we can reduce it where possible and ensure that it doesn't take hold. It is a good idea, when you are getting to know exactly what clutter you have (see page 20) to make a mental note of the sources of the clutter that enters your home. Although there are many sources common to everyone – supermarkets, clothes shops, advertisers – each household will have its own particular areas of concern. There will also be differing degrees for everyone as to the amount of clutter that a source causes. The young family, for example, will get more junk mail adverts about mortgages and loans than a single pensioner – but we will all get communications about taxation.

We need to be aware of the places that we must avoid in order to dodge the clutter. For you, it may be car-boot sales where you will buy someone else's junk or the seasonal sales in clothes shops where you will buy yet another pair of black trousers or just one more shirt to go with them. Or it may be the craft supplies shop where you just cannot resist the dinky little what-nots that will be ideal for a craft project you haven't planned yet. Perhaps you find it difficult to resist sending off for catalogues full of all sorts of exciting things – and then ordering from them. Buying books on the Internet can be a stumbling block for many people and, if you're the sort of person who can never bear to let a book go (even when you've read it and didn't particularly like it), your bookshelves will soon be cluttered and groaning.

Think carefully about where your clutter came from and about your own particular weak points. This knowledge will help you not only when you are tackling the initial task of decluttering but also when you are trying to keep a decluttered area tidy and organized.

Places to avoid

Some places and events are just waiting to thrust clutter at you. If you find you are easily tempted to add to your existing clutter, don't go anywhere near car-boot sales, charity shops, seaside gift shops, or 'massive sales' in any sort of shop.

Car-boot sales

Car-boot sales can be a mixture of other declutterers selling their own junk and businesses selling items cheaply. Other people's junk can be strangely seductive. It can be an interesting way to spend a weekend morning, browsing through the things that other people are throwing away. You can gasp at how awful some people's taste is or wonder whether they ever used that antique teapot and did they have cups and saucers to match. However, if your idle interest turns to thoughts like, 'That's nice – and so cheap!' get away, as fast as you can. Unless the item in question is beautiful or extremely useful and could find a valuable place in your life, all you will be doing is adding to your decluttering task – and wasting money. Of course, the test of beauty or usefulness should be the one we set whenever we're considering any purchase but somehow, all reason can desert us at car-boot sales.

figure 13 a car-boot sale

Charity shops

There is a similar scenario at charity shops as at car-boot sales. The designer evening dress at a bargain-basement price will not be anything but clutter when you get it home if you don't have an occasion on which to wear it. The handful of second-hand books may be a bargain but don't you already have plenty of books? If you have got lots of books but you've read them all so you need something to read in bed – or wherever – then why haven't you brought some of your own books to the charity shop? If you brought ten books into the shop and then bought five, not only would the charity benefit but you will have started on decluttering your bookshelves.

Sales

Cut-price sales in any sort of shop present a temptation to collect clutter. Just remember that if it doesn't fit you, you are not going to wear it (and you are highly unlikely to slim into it either), and if you don't have a lawn then the mower at a knock-down price is simply junk. Ask yourself whether you would have bought the item at the full price. If the answer is no, think very carefully about why you want to buy it now. If the price is the most attractive aspect, don't buy it. Be sure that the item you are thinking of buying will be used or admired and that it will have a genuine place in your life. Of course, you will know better what you need to buy after you have completed your decluttering project. If you have just organized your wardrobe and found that you have two pairs of white jeans or three bright pink T-shirts, then you will not even look at the white jeans or pink T-shirts when you go into a clothes shop. If you find that there is something that you really need concentrate on that, but you may not have a clear picture of your needs until you've stripped away the clutter.

Developing a strict policy of one in, one out will help you to keep these danger areas under control. If you never buy a book on the Internet without giving away one of your books first, you will always have space on your bookshelves but will not be depriving yourself of new books. Similarly, if you only go clothes shopping when you know exactly what you need because you've just thrown out or given away at least one item, then your wardrobe will remain organized. This one in, one out policy will, in conjunction with an awareness of your own areas of weakness, ensure that you do not succumb to the danger areas.

Five things to do instead of shopping

If you are a shopaholic and continually bringing more clutter into your home – whether it is from clothes shops, department store sales, car-boot sales or charity shops – here are five things that you could try doing when you feel the urge to go shopping:

1 Repair and clean clothes so that they will always be ready to wear – then you may not need to go and buy more.
2 Sort through your make-up and toiletries. You may find that you have more than you thought. Throw away the old items and bring into use all the unopened items you've been buying but not using.
3 Empty all the unopened shopping bags from previous retail therapy trips. If you have even one item still in the bag and

unused, you need to cut down on the amount of shopping trips you make. Use what you've got.

4 Gather up all the loose change from the different points in your home where it has been abandoned, no matter who has left it there. Put it in a savings box and plan what you – as a family – will do with it when you get to a certain amount.

5 Clean out and polish all your handbags and shoes. You'll get more use out of them if they are taken care of and you may find you don't need to buy any more.

Gift clutter

The important thing to remember about gifts is that you do not have to keep them forever. We often hang on to things that have very kindly been given to us even though we don't like them, they don't fit in with our lifestyle, and there is no way that we would ever have chosen them for ourselves. Guilt means that we feel that to throw or give away a gift item is somehow an insult to the person who gave it to us. So we hang on to all sorts of things out of a sense of loyalty to the giver.

The task is to separate the feelings you have for the giver from the feelings you have about the gift. Giving away (or selling) an unwanted gift does not alter your feelings for the person who gave it to you. You can hate the gift and still love them. The other thing we should keep in mind is that, to the people who really love us, it will be more important that we are happy than that we keep their gift. Clutter does not induce a feeling of well-being so you have to let it go – gift or not.

The options for letting gifts go are similar to those for any clutter. You can give it away, sell it, donate it or throw it away. As unwanted gifts will usually be in a new condition and may still have the original box or wrappings, there will often be opportunities to sell the gift. Car-boot sales (remember to go to sell – not to buy – or you'll end up with more clutter), the Internet and small ads in the paper can all come in handy as outlets for your superfluous gifts. If you look at the gift and know that it is not to your taste but that it would be ideal for someone you know, check with them whether they want it or, if you are unable to see who might want such a thing, donate it to charity. You would be surprised at what can be sold in a charity shop. There is a buyer out there for just about everything, so make a donation. If all else fails, you will have to throw the item away – but don't hang on to it because of guilty feelings.

When you've got rid of all the gifts that had become clutter, try not to impose a similar problem on your friends and family. When giving a gift, make sure that it is something they really want. If in any doubt about what to get, ask. And remember, the gift is for the person you're giving it to, so it should please them, not you. This principle can also help you to stay clutter-free in the future if you pass on the idea to your friends and family. If you can let them know just what you would like to receive for a birthday, Christmas or other celebration, you won't have the problem of what to do with unwanted gifts ever again. It also helps if they understand that your aim is to remain free of clutter.

Why are you keeping all your clutter?

The main reasons for hanging on to junk are fear, broken dreams and guilt. Sometimes there is also an element of not finding time to do the job – we all lead busy lives – but there is usually a deeper, more difficult reason for keeping our clutter. For example, it could be that we are anxious about hurting other people's feelings so we hold on to things that mean something to others but no longer fit our own lives, or because it was a gift and it would be hurtful to throw it away.

Fear

Fear stops us from throwing away all sorts of clutter. We keep 'fat clothes' when we've lost weight because we're afraid that we'll put the weight back on. We hang on to all types of gadgets and tools because they might come in handy – that is a fear of what might happen. We don't pass on pieces of paper for someone else to deal with because we're afraid that they won't be able to do as good a job as we might have done. We fear regret or making mistakes, and this can hold us back from doing all sorts of things. Fear can paralyze us so that we are unable to make even the simplest of decisions. To overcome this, we need to take a more positive approach to making decisions. We need to see the good things that can come out of making the decision – the advantages that can come with a clutter-free home.

Broken dreams

Broken dreams can encompass a variety of junk too. We hold on to things because we don't want to acknowledge that we have moved on and, instead of embracing change, we resist it by clinging to our old ways and our old clutter. This clutter could include hobbies that we no longer enjoy. Perhaps we dreamed of becoming an expert seamstress one day but we weren't quite as good as we hoped and so abandoned the idea – but still we hang on to the pieces of fabric, the patterns, the trimmings, the sewing machine and all the things that are necessary to do a proper job. This type of clutter could also include memorabilia from previous relationships. Perhaps that dress that you wore on your first date with your ex-husband was important to you once, but if your ex is no longer a part of your life, then the dress certainly shouldn't be – especially if it no longer fits and it's been out of fashion for years. Some people hang on to the stuff of broken dreams because they are important memories but the clutter isn't the memory – the memory is in your mind and will stay there long after you've sent the clothes to the charity shop or thrown the memorabilia in the bin.

Guilt

Many things can induce guilt. Gifts are a particularly problematical area but, remember, once something has been given to you it's yours – yours to do what you please with. Expensive items that we have treated ourselves to are another area for guilty feelings. We feel guilty that we spent so much on an item that we don't use, so we hang on to it. But if it's never used or admired or enjoyed, keeping it will only serve to remind us of our folly in buying it. Let it go and forget it.

We would find it much easier to let go of most of the clutter that we accumulate because of broken dreams, feelings of fear and guilt if we acknowledged that things change. Life changes and the people in your life will change, your interests will change. We should welcome these changes and accept that the things we need will also change. When our needs change, there will be an opportunity to declutter.

Top ten excuses for not decluttering

Count how many of these excuses you've used:

1   I might need it someday – that may or may not be true but in the meantime, while you're taking a chance on that, you're having to store it, clean it, clean around it, and take care of it.

2   It's handmade – unless you love it or use it regularly, this is irrelevant.

3   It was a gift – don't let guilt stop you from living your life as you want to live it.

4   It was expensive – you've paid for it once, don't keep paying for it by letting it hang around reminding you of your extravagance.

5   I'm going to fix it – you won't.

6   It will fit me when I lose weight – if and when you lose weight, you'll want to treat yourself to new clothes.

7   As soon as I throw it out, I'll need it – ask yourself when you last needed it. If it's a while, the chances are you won't ever need it.

8   It might come back into fashion – fashion changes and next time loon pants or sparkly jackets come into fashion there will be just a little something different about them.

9   I used to love it – if you don't love it anymore then it doesn't deserve a place in your life now.

10 It was a bargain – admit you made a mistake (a cheap one) and throw it out.

Guilty feelings

We shouldn't feel guilty about throwing out or passing on any of our possessions. If they are ours, we are free to do exactly what we like with them. We own our clutter, it doesn't own us.

In today's society, we are encouraged to constantly strive to have more – to buy more, to get more – and this is more stuff. It is a materialistic world and we go along with it, working longer and longer hours at more and more stressful jobs, and for what? Often we do it to be able to buy yet another pair of shoes or more furniture or more gadgets. All this new stuff is added to our old stuff and it builds up. It needs caring for, cleaning, storing and protecting. It demands our time and our commitment. And all this at a time when what we really need is more time, more space, less stress and peace of mind. By perpetuating the notion that we need to acquire more and more things rather than more time and space for ourselves, we are denying ourselves a quality of life. We tie ourselves up with getting the things we think we need and then we feel guilty about them.

Don't let the main use of your time be caring for your clutter – moving it around, cleaning it, making decisions about it – when you could be spending your time and money on caring for yourself and the people who matter to you. Use the time you save by not having too much stuff on playing with your children or having lunch with a friend. Use the money you save on not buying more junk on having an exciting holiday with your partner.

Consider this. The freedom that you will feel when you are clutter-free, when the weight of all that junk has been released from around your neck and you are free to enjoy your home, your time and your life will be far, far greater than the guilt you feel at throwing things out.

Summary

In this chapter you have:

- Become more aware of how your clutter has built up.
- Learned about the places you may visit and the situations you may find yourself in where you will be vulnerable to more clutter – car-boot sales, charity shops and cut-price sales in shops of all types. When you are sensitive to the dangers, you can take steps to avoid collecting more junk.
- Found out five suggestions for what you can do instead of going shopping for more stuff.
- Recognized why unwanted gifts cause clutter problems and found out how to deal with them.
- Learned why you are keeping your clutter – because of fear, guilt or broken dreams.
- Been given the top ten excuses for not decluttering – how many of these have you found yourself using?
- Acknowledged your ownership of your clutter and that you are free to do exactly what you like with it.

Action plan

Now that you know what your danger areas are, you should plan to tackle some of them right away:

- Get charitable. Take a bag and collect five items from your home that would be suitable for your favourite charity shop – concentrate on unwanted gift items.

- Commit yourself to a policy of one in, one out – do not bring anything into your home unless you can let something else go. This is an especially effective tactic if you can relate the two items. For example, only buy a pair of trousers if you can remove an old pair from your wardrobe.

- Next time you feel the need for a spot of retail therapy, choose one of the suggested tasks given on page 168 to distract you.

- Write down why you are hanging on to your clutter – are any of your reasons in the top ten excuses for not decluttering given on page 172?

14

life after decluttering

In this chapter you will learn:
- how it will feel when you get organized
- the benefits of decluttering – and staying that way
- how to keep it up.

Reaching your goal

Well, you've got there. If you've worked your way through this book and decluttered all the areas of your home and your life that needed it, you will now have a beautifully organized home which contains all the things that are important to you and which will allow you to lead your life as you want to. It will have been hard work but the benefits are enormous. You no longer need a bigger house, a bigger car or a bigger wardrobe as the possessions you have will now fit into the space you already have.

The most important thing to remember now that you've reached your goal is that you must not go back to your old ways. If you do what you've always done, you will get what you've always got. So, don't be tempted to buy more things to fill up the space you have created. Just enjoy the space in your home and in your mind. Don't waste time on regrets. The past is not where we live; it is where we used to live and we should learn from it.

The benefits

Recall the advantages. This is a little like counting your blessings – always a useful, rewarding exercise. Give yourself time to gloat about the benefits of a decluttered life. You will feel so much better than you ever anticipated that you really should spend time on understanding just how far you have come. Think back to how cluttered your life was, visualize each of the spaces that you have worked on as they were before all your hard work. Recall each room and cupboard. If your visualization skills are lacking, have a walk around your home now and check out the organized drawers and cupboards, revel in the fact that you can see plenty of clear floor space in each room where maybe there was none before. Slip your hand into your wardrobe – do the hangers move freely with the clothes not being squashed and creased, with all the same type of clothes stored together, ready for action? Check your utensil drawer in the kitchen. Can you find what you want at a glance when before your hard work everything was simply an impenetrable jumble? Pop your head around the shed door. Can you now lay your hands on your box of seeds or your hand tools straight away when it may have cost you many minutes of frustrated searching prior to your decluttering exercise? Is there room in your garage for a car now? Imagine that you have to move house in a hurry. Wouldn't it have taken you much longer to pack up and go when you had so much more useless stuff in your home?

Then think about the things that have been removed. Did you manage to sell some items that no longer had a place in your life and, if so, how much money did you make? Quickly add up all the bags and boxes of rubbish that you have removed from your home and visualize them all in one awful pile – a mountain of rubbish. Aren't you glad now that this is no longer in your home?

Recall the four major advantages that your newly decluttered life now has:

1 You have space. Space is the best reward for all that hard work. There will be space in your cupboards and drawers, space in your wardrobe and, more important than that, there will be space in your life. This space will give you room to breathe and to think. There will be space to display the precious (to you) objects that you have made a conscious decision to keep. Revel in all that space and the wonderfully free feeling that it will give you.

2 You will feel better. No longer will you have to explain and find excuses for the mess in your home. You will feel proud of your space and released from the burden the junk had become. An added benefit is that people may start to treat you differently. They will respect you and your space because they can see that you have self-respect and are worthy of their respect.

3 You will have more time to do the things you really want to do. When you have stopped looking after all your clutter, you will find that you have spare time and also the lighter feeling that goes with being free of clutter; this will allow you to do exactly what matters to you. When you have stopped finding your way through rubbish in your home, searching for things on a daily basis and saved the time you used to spend cleaning the clutter – and around it – you will be free to decide how you live your life. How will you spend your extra time?

4 You will save money. When you know exactly what you have and can lay your hands on it immediately, you will no longer buy things you don't need simply because you don't know that you already have one or because you can't find it. The feeling of freedom that you get from finally becoming

decluttered will mean that you never want to go back to your previous, junk-ridden state, and you will no longer want to spend vast quantities of money on acquiring 'stuff'.

You will have noticed that clearing your clutter has a cumulative effect. The first step feels great, the next step shows you how far you can go and the improvements that are possible in your life, and the final step – when you've reached the end of your first decluttering journey – will make you feel fantastic. It's a great achievement to go from cluttered to clear, and you will have seen the following improvements along the way:

- When you've cleared one cupboard – you'll now have somewhere to put the clutter that accumulates on the floor.
- When you've cleared a whole room – you'll now have a place to relax, free of the constant 'chatter' of messy junk.
- When you've cleared your whole house – you'll have more time for what you really want to do with your life.

If you've worked your way through this book and tackled all your clutter demons, you will now be taking advantage of all the benefits of a clutter-free life. You'll be moving forward in your life, unhampered by the weight of all that stuff and will be feeling in control, less stressed and more relaxed. Who could ask for more? Well, you really want this feeling to last forever. For that, you will need to continue your decluttering journey. It won't be as hard now that you have got your possessions under control, but you will need to be ever-vigilant to avoid slipping back into the habits that got you into trouble in the first place.

Keeping it up

You will feel wonderful when you've got rid of all that clutter and your home looks tidy, comfortable and organized, but if you don't keep decluttering in mind, you will soon be back to square one. All those things that made up your clutter before will start to creep back into your home. You'll buy more books and keep stuffing them into every available space on your bookshelves. You'll lose weight and buy smaller clothes but then hang on to your 'fat' clothes 'just in case'. You'll soon accumulate another pile of household bills and papers to replace the one you've sorted and thrown out. So, the only solution is to keep it up! Here are a few things that you should get into the habit of doing to keep up the good work:

figure 14 a well-organized living room and joining dining room

- Spend just a few minutes – perhaps five or ten – every morning on a quick pick-up routine. Take a box or a basket and go through your main rooms quickly, picking things up if they are not in the right place and, as you move from room to room, drop them off where they belong. You will be surprised by how much tidier your home will look the whole time with even a very small, daily blitz like this.

- Make sure you deal with things such as the morning mail when they are in your hand. If you don't change the habit of putting things like this down on kitchen worktops or the coffee table, you will soon feel cluttered again. Put dates in the diary straight away, pay bills and file them, recycle junk mail immediately. If you really can't deal with everything as soon as you get it, have a basket hidden away where you can put correspondence until the appropriate time.

- Take care if you go into charity shops or to car-boot sales. Unless it is perfect for you, don't be tempted by lots of cheap items because they won't be a bargain if they simply become junk.

- Get your family into the habit of putting things away. Make it a rule that everyone must put away all the bits from one activity before they are allowed to start on another. This is a change that can be brought about in any family and – once it's ingrained – tidiness will be something that is a useful trait throughout life. However, it will take time and plenty of reminders before it becomes automatic for everyone in the household to put their things away.

- Sort out your magazines every week or month – don't wait until you have a pile teetering in the corner of your living room. Tear out any articles or recipes that you want to keep and file them away, then discard the magazine. Either give the magazine to a friend, your doctor or dentist or put it in the recycling bin.

- Operate a policy of one in, one out. If you buy a new pair of black trousers, throw a pair out. Before you buy anything at all, ask yourself if you really need it.

- Check out your clothes as the seasons change. When it gets cooler and you start to bring sweaters out of storage or when you need some lighter weight clothes in the summer, this is the perfect time to review what you have and have a quick decluttering session. Throw out anything you haven't worn that season and which will not suit the following season. Pack away clothes that you want to keep for next season.

- Think back to what your trouble spots were before you successfully decluttered your home and then pay special attention to these areas to avoid clutter creeping back in.
- Go public. Let your family and friends know that you have adopted a new lifestyle. This will not only engender envy and respect, it will also help to ensure that they do not re-clutter your space with gifts of the same sort that you have just thrown out. When your birthday, anniversary or Christmas comes around, be sure to let them know exactly what you would like to receive. This will make their job as present buyer easier and they will probably be grateful for the help.
- Recall why you decluttered in the first place. Aren't you saving time and money, feeling less stressed and more organised? Why would you want to go back to your cluttered, disorganised existence?
- Remember that everything costs something to maintain – and in the case of clutter you often pay with your quality of life, and with your time and energy.
- Only you can decide what is junk in your life and what is not. If it gives you pleasure to look at or to use, even if it is the ugliest thing on earth, then it is not junk. Similarly, a really beautiful thing can be junk if no one loves it.

Now give yourself a pat on the back!

Summary

In this chapter you have:

- Reviewed the advantages of having successfully decluttered. The main ones being more space, a feeling of satisfaction and control, and more time and money.
- Learned some ways to keep your clutter under control by developing habits such as a quick pick-up every morning, dealing with mail as it arrives, regularly sorting out magazines, checking clothes at the start of every season and operating a policy of one in, one out.

Action plan

Now, you've done the hard work and will probably be sitting back enjoying the fruits of your labour. Don't rest for too long because it is worryingly easy to allow clutter to creep back into your life. To maintain the feeling of control that being clutter-free gives you, it is vital that you develop habits and routines. Try the following and build them into your daily life:

- Gloat a little. Go to the areas in your home where your decluttering has been particularly successful and compare how things are now with how things were before you started your decluttering journey. Go to your child's room and check out the storage – hopefully they're putting things away and all their toys and clothes are readily available to them. Or give yourself a pat on the back when you park your car in the garage – something you couldn't do before.

- As soon as you're dressed and are ready to face the day, make the rounds of your living space and pick up anything that is not where it should be. Remove mugs and plates that someone used for a late night snack in the living room and take them to the kitchen. Pick up the school bag from the kitchen and place it ready near the front door. Take the tennis racket left near the front door and drop it off in your child's room. Don't allow this routine to take more than five or ten minutes each day and follow the next action point to ensure that this task does not get out of hand.

- Set the rule now that everyone is responsible for putting away the things they have used. You will then have to persevere until everyone in the family has taken this on board.

- Review your shopping habits. Before you go, check what you are intending to buy is genuinely needed and that you are operating a policy of one in, one out.

- Throw an 'I'm decluttered and proud' party. This will give you the opportunity to let your family and friends know about your new goals and also to celebrate your success, basking in their admiration of how far you've come. It might also deter unwanted gifts in the future.

- Remember what life was like before, when you couldn't find anything, drawers wouldn't close, you were ashamed to invite people into your home, and clutter was draining your time and energy? Resolve never to go back.

taking it further

Useful organizations

Book Aid
Recycle books to developing countries. Check website first for criteria
Tel: 0207 733 3577
www.bookaid.org

British Association of Removers
Find a local removal company
www.removers.org.uk

Computer Aid
Non-profit supplier of computers to developing countries
Tel: 0207 281 0091
www.computeraid.org

Cruse
Support for bereaved people
www.crusebereavementcare.org.uk

Furniture Reuse
National co-ordinating body for furniture reuse schemes
Tel: 0117 954 3571
www.frn.org.uk

Mailing Preference Service
DMA House
70 Margaret Street
London W1W 8SS
Tel: 0845 703 4599
www.mpsonline.org.uk

Oxfam
Operates a mobile phone recycling scheme. Take mobile phones into any Oxfam shop
www.oxfam.org.uk

Scope UK
Operates a computer recycling scheme to raise money for cerebral palsy charity
Tel: 01757 708180
www.scope.org.uk

Telephone Preference Service
Address and telephone number as above
www.tpsonline.org.uk

Vision Aid Overseas
Recycle spectacles. UK-based charity helping needy people overseas who suffer from poor eyesight
Tel: 01293 535016
www.vao.org.uk

Waste Connect UK
Lots of information about recycling (including locating your nearest recycling point)
www.wasteconnect.co.uk

Useful websites

www.amazon.co.uk or www.amazon.com
Website with section for selling second-hand books

www.argos.co.uk
Retailer of storage products and furniture

www.cotswoldco.com
Retailer of storage products and furniture

www.diy.co.uk
B&Q's website – retailer of DIY items and gardening products

www.ebay.co.uk or www.ebay.com
Auction website

www.focusdiy.co.uk
Retailer of DIY items

www.heals.co.uk
Retailer of furniture and storage items

www.homebase.co.uk
Retailer of DIY and gardening products

www.homesources.co.uk
Guide to UK suppliers of fitted furniture and other products

www.thehousecoach.com
Advice to help present your house for sale

index